PUNKROCKER HR

Turning up the Volume on Humanity at Work

By: John Englehart Jr. MDE, SHRM-CP

ISBN: 979-8-218-83443-2

Printed in the United States of America
First Edition

Legal Notice

Author Contact: JohnEnglehartJr@proton.me

Dedication:

I want to thank my Lord and Savior, Jesus Christ, for blessing me with the ability to write this book. I haven't always gotten it right, but He has never stopped being faithful to me.

To the many friends and coworkers, I've had the privilege to work with over the years, you've all shaped me in ways I can't begin to explain.

I also want to thank my wife, Sharon and my children, Zoey and Brooks. They are my greatest inspiration, and I dedicate this book to them. Thank you for loving me through all my flaws and cheering me on when I doubted myself.

Table of Contents:

Prologue: The Sneezer

Before jumping into the book you're about to read, I wanted to start with a lighthearted story, one that perfectly captures what it's like being a dad while trying to write something as personal as this book.

A few weeks before publishing, my daughter Zoey, now a freshman in high school, told us she'd be performing in an evening concert with the instrumental band. This was one of her first big performances, so she was excited but a little nervous. She asked if we could be there, and of course, the answer was yes.

My wife had another commitment that night, so it was just me and my 10-year-old son, Brooks, in the audience from our family. The high school auditorium was huge, probably 250 seats or more, and had that classic pre-concert energy: parents whispering, kids warming up, instruments squeaking and tuning. Brooks and I grabbed seats in the middle section, about ten rows back.

We spotted Zoey easily. She was sitting upright, clarinet in hand, trying her best to look calm, but I could tell she was nervous. And honestly, I was nervous for her too. There's just something about watching your kid step into a moment they've prepared for.
After a few minutes, the lights dimmed and the chatter faded into silence. The band director raised his hands, the universal sign that the performance was about to begin. It was so quiet you could hear a pin drop.

And that's when it happened. I felt a sneeze coming on.

Now, let me preface this by admitting something important: I come from a long line of loud sneezers. The kind of sneezers who make strangers flinch. The kind who trigger car alarms. That kind.

I did everything I could to stop it. I tickled my nose. I took a big gulp of soda. I held my breath. I prayed the band would start playing and drown out the coming explosion.

I looked at Brooks, eyes watering. He looked at me and slowly shook his head, silently pleading, "Dad...not now." But it was too late.

ACHOO!

The sneeze echoed through the entire auditorium. Half the audience turned to look at me. A little girl in the row in front of us even popped her head up and said, "God bless you!" in the sweetest voice imaginable. I wish that had been the end of it. But no.

Sneeze #2 was loading.

I looked at Brooks again. He braced for impact.

ACHOO!

Even louder this time. Now *everyone* was looking at me, most of them half laughing. I can see the humor now, but in the moment? Absolute parental nightmare.

And then, because life has a sense of humor, I felt a third sneeze coming.

A triple sneeze. Unprecedented.

Before I could even process it…

ACHOO!

The third sneeze practically rattled the auditorium. Even the instrumental band looked up. Zoey, sitting in the third row, spotted me and her face froze in horror. To make things worse, the band director turned *to me* and said, "God bless you!"

The entire auditorium erupted in laughter.

And then, right on cue, the band began playing. If only they'd started ten seconds earlier.

After the performance, parents crowded into the back of the auditorium to pick up their kids. Zoey walked up, and I hugged her and told her how proud I was.

Right then, one of her bandmates looked at me and said to Zoey: "Wait…is that your dad? Was he the super sneezer tonight?"

Zoey froze. I could see the conflict on her face. Does she claim me? Or pretend I'm just some long lost Uncle giving her a ride home?

Before she could answer, an older man behind me suddenly let out a sneeze so thunderous it nearly blew my hat off.

"God bless you!" Zoey's friend said.

She leaned toward Zoey and whispered, "Never mind. It must've been that dude. I'd be so embarrassed if that was my dad."

Zoey, without missing a beat, said, "Me too." And then she gave me the smallest sideways smile. We laughed about it on the way home.

I share this story because I'm learning something as my kids grow: the things I say and do, big or small, serious or ridiculous, always land on them in some way. And as I started thinking about publishing this book, a book that includes some deeply personal stories (including the one in Chapter 1), I knew I had to be thoughtful about how it would affect them too.

So, I sat down with both Zoey and Brooks and let them read the heavy parts and the lighthearted parts. Then I waited, holding my breath, wondering what they'd say. Instead of hesitation or fear, they both hugged me and said, "We love you. We're proud of you. You should publish this."

I don't want to steal any thunder from the introduction or the chapters that follow by saying too much here, but I needed to share how I obtained their blessing first. This book isn't just my story. It's ours. And with their hugs, they were all in.

Let the story begin…

Introduction:

A Different Type of Book

One of my favorite movies is *Forrest Gump,* the story of an ordinary man with an extraordinary heart who quietly changes the world. I love it because it feels less like a movie and more like a conversation. Forrest simply sits on a bench and tells a collection of stories from his life, each one powerful on its own, but together they paint a much bigger picture. Each story, whether it's his run across America or his shrimp business, stands alone, but together they create something unforgettable.

That's the best way to describe this book. Think of it as a conversation between two friends. Over the past decade, I've been writing articles and essays, sometimes for social media, sometimes for a blog, sometimes just for myself, about my work and life experiences. After sharing them with family, friends, and a few coworkers, I usually let the writings go and moved on. I had no idea then that those articles would eventually come together here forming one larger story that needs to be told.

Here's why this book matters now: the workplace is changing fast. Millennials are stepping into leadership, Gen Z is reshaping the culture, and burnout, disengagement, and mistrust are at record highs. Today's workforce wants to be treated like human beings, not as headcount to be managed or an input on a spreadsheet, but as people with stories, struggles, and hopes of their own. The truth is, every employee and every customer carries something unseen, a weight they bring with them each day. We may not always see that story, but if we choose to lead with humanity, we start to see the person first. That simple shift changes everything, how we treat our teams, and how our teams, in turn, treat our customers.

I won't fully define PunkRocker HR just yet, but if I were in an elevator with Elon Musk and had 30 seconds to explain why it matters, here's the mission statement:

> "PunkRocker HR is about turning up the volume on humanity in the workplace, challenging transactional practices with curiosity, leading with empathy and hope, and fighting for balance, so people can find purpose at work and still have peace at home."

> If he asked, "Why do you call it *PunkRocker HR?*"

> I would say, "You'll have to buy the book to find that out."

You'll hear me refer to Transactional HR often in this book. It's an important part of the work we do and has been for decades. Transactional HR focuses on the forms, processes, and compliance work that keep organizations running—necessary and valuable but often centered more on systems than people. However, Transactional HR alone will not help us meet the demands of today's changing workforce.

I should probably apologize in advance; you're going to see me use a lot of sports metaphors in this book. It's how my brain works, and it's the best way I can explain the difference between Transactional HR and PunkRocker HR. Take, for example, a major league pitcher with a great fastball. Transactional HR is like fastball. But the fastball alone won't carry you through an entire career—you need other pitches in your arsenal, like a curveball or a changeup, to stay effective and keep evolving. That's where PunkRocker HR comes in, as your expanded pitch arsenal for long-term success. This book will explore how PunkRocker HR, when applied, can help you meet the needs of today's evolving workplace and workforce.

When I first shared the title of this book, *PunkRocker HR*, with my wife, she gave me that look. The one that says, "I think you'll eventually come up with a better name." But as you'll read in Chapter One, the title was inspired partly by a movie a friend mentioned in a text, and partly by the spirit of punk itself, daring to do things differently, challenging the status quo, and not being afraid to stand out. When I explained that, she just rolled her eyes. But in my own PunkRocker way, I stuck with it.

This book is very different from a typical self-help or leadership book, and that's on purpose. It's a collection of essays and reflections, each written at a different stage of my career, connected by recurring themes that trace my growth as a leader and a person. While the themes may overlap and even feel repetitive at times, that's by design; each story adds a new angle or "golden nugget" to what PunkRocker HR looks like in action.

At its core, this book is a story, one that begins in a place where I experienced what it's like to have the volume on humanity turned all the way down and to feel the weight of failure. But as the story unfolds, it becomes about rediscovering hope, faith, and a way to lead that turns that volume back up, not just in the workplace, but in life.

The stories trace my journey, from delivering mail for the United States Postal Service, to moving into HR and then serving in HR at other organizations. Each piece reflects where I was at the time, what I was wrestling with, and what I was learning. Writing has always been my safe space, the place where I felt most comfortable expressing myself. Writing lets me say what's truly in my heart in a way speaking never could.

Someone recently asked me if this book was going to be a collection of my victories and successes. The answer is quite the opposite. This book is more about my failures. The truth is, I've learned far more about myself as a leader, a father, a husband, and a friend through failure. It was in the moments when I felt broken, misunderstood, or lost that I discovered who I really was, and who I wanted to be. My hope is that somewhere in these pages, at least one story will resonate with you, encourage you, or even challenge you in how you approach leadership, HR, work, and life.

Who is this Book Intended For?

Thank you for not letting the "HR" in the title scare you off. Whether you're a leader, an emerging leader, an HR professional, or simply someone looking for inspiration for the next step in your career, this book is for you. While it takes a hard look at how HR is often approached, the lessons reach far beyond the HR world and apply to anyone who wants to grow. In the end, this book is for humans who want to be better humans in the workplace.

Think of an organization as a body. For example, in a university: Professors might claim to be the "brains," driving knowledge and research. Students could be the lifeblood, pulsing with potential. Facilities staff might be the backbone, keeping the campus standing strong. Admissions and student services could be the eyes and ears, welcoming and guiding. Marketing and communications would be the voice, shaping the institution's story. In my opinion, HR is the "heart" of the university. HR pumps the blood, empathy, support, and humanity into every part, like helping to hire the right faculty to teach or meeting the needs of staff so they can thrive, which all in turn helps students to learn. If the heart falters, the entire institution struggles.

That's why this book will help you regardless of your background. An honest review of the heart of every organization and how we keep it strong and healthy can benefit every leader, every HR professional, and every professional searching for their path forward.

For the HR Pros:

If you are reading this as an HR professional, I want to be clear about what this book is and is not. It is not a critique of HR professionals or the profession in general. By all means, we're in this together. Think of this book as a conversation at an HR retreat and the topic is: "How can we do HR better?" It's a chance to reset how we see our work and rediscover our purpose.

A lot of what we've done has worked well for a long time, but now we're facing a new generational mix and new expectations. My hope is that this book adds a spark of "hey, let's try that" for our profession. So, join me in the conversation, because the future of HR is something we get to shape together. And part of shaping that future means remembering why we chose HR in the first place or maybe remembering how HR chose us.

As I wrote this book, I thought about this: I don't know anyone who ever said that as a young child, their dream was to work in HR. For me, my dream was to replace Cal Ripken Jr[1]. at shortstop for the Baltimore Orioles. Unfortunately, I couldn't hit a curve ball very well. Chances are, you had other dreams as well. Yet something

---

[1] Cal Ripken Jr., nicknamed "The Iron Man," is a Hall of Fame shortstop and third baseman who played 21 seasons for the Baltimore Orioles. He's best known for his record-breaking streak of 2,632 consecutive games, surpassing Lou Gehrig's long-standing record.

along the way either pushed or inspired you to take a chance on a career in HR. Writing these stories as well as writing this book has helped me revisit why I decided to do HR and helped to find that spark again. Hopefully, it will do the same for you.

Thank You

Thank you for giving this book a chance and having this conversation with me. My prayer is that you'll find encouragement in these pages. Your story matters. You have a bigger role in the lives of others than you may ever realize. If you've ever felt like giving up, or if you've ever been told you don't belong, then this book is for you.

This book begins in a tough place, with the story of how I felt like a failure. But it doesn't stay there. It ends in a different place: one of hope, healing, and the discovery of what I now call PunkRocker HR. Walk with me through the ups and downs, the failures and lessons, and maybe by the end, you'll see pieces of your own story in mine.

Author's Note

These stories are drawn from my own experiences and reflections. They're meant to share what I learned along the way, not to cast blame, but to show how even the toughest moments can teach us something.

Chapter 1: Field of Dreams

The Career Climb

After graduating from high school, I joined the U.S. Postal Service as an 18-year-old mailman. After ten years of delivering mail and serving as a supervisor, I took a detail in HR and fell in love with the work. I spent the next decade in HR roles at the Postal Service before moving into other organizations, while always bringing my own unique approach to the job.

I love HR work. You really have to love it to do it well for a long time. I got into HR 15 years ago because I wanted to help people and bring positive energy and creativity into the workplace. During my time as a postal worker, I saw how "personnel" could feel impersonal, and I wanted to change that. Why not bring energy and hope into everything we do in HR, whether it's something as dry as workers' compensation or as exciting as talent acquisition?

The best way to describe my leadership and HR style is this: HR grounded in empathy, compassion, and coaching, built on a strong belief in dignity and humanity at work. Over the years, I saw how some leaders treated employees and promised myself I would never ask anyone to do, or do to anyone, what I wouldn't want done to me. The golden rule that Christ taught has always guided me as both a leader and an HR professional:

"Do to others as you would have them do to you[2]."

---

[2] Luke 6:31 (NIV)

I'm not saying I hit the mark on this approach every time, but I did my best. Sometimes that meant pushing back against relying only on "Transactional HR" and leaning into a more human-centered defense of people. I also tried to weave in humor and positivity wherever I could, knowing that work can be heavy and people sometimes just need permission to breathe and laugh.

As my HR career progressed across different organizations, one part of my job stayed the same: preparing leaders for the changing workforce. I spent a lot of time talking about what was coming, how Millennials, Gen Z, and soon Gen Alpha would bring new expectations. We needed to adapt while still honoring the roots of the culture that had served the organization well for decades. In one strategic planning session, I even showed up dressed as Doc Brown from *Back to the Future*[3] to spark conversation about what the future workforce might look like, and how we could embrace generational differences instead of resisting them. My goal wasn't to disrupt but to help us look inward so we could make the changes needed to thrive.

Along the way, I championed the idea that a "trust and inspire[4]" leadership style might often have more impact than a traditional "command and control" approach with these incoming generations. Many leaders leaned in, but for a select few, the shift felt unfamiliar. And I understood that; even positive change can feel uncomfortable.

---

[3] Back to the Future (1985) – A sci-fi comedy directed by Robert Zemeckis, starring Michael J. Fox as teenager Marty McFly and Christopher Lloyd as the eccentric inventor Doc Brown. Marty accidentally travels back to 1955 in Doc's time-traveling DeLorean and has to fix the past to make sure his future still exists.
[4] Trust & Inspire – A 2022 leadership book by Stephen M.R. Covey that contrasts "command and control" leadership with a new approach built on trust, inspiration, and empowerment.

Life-Changing Role

In this book, I'll be focusing on one particular HR leadership role and the events that followed, because they changed my life forever. In this role, I was blessed to work at an excellent organization filled with talented people who loved their work and the customers they served. I loved leading my young HR team. I had the chance to mentor them, watch them grow, and see them accomplish great things. I cared about each of them, not just as employees but as people. The work wasn't always easy, and I never took their commitment for granted.

One of my favorite memories was hosting them at my home for a holiday party, watching them laugh around the Christmas tree while my heart was full. Moments like that reminded me that leadership isn't about policies and processes. It's about people. That respect and gratitude never faded.

For a while, I was also blessed to work under a great boss, someone with decades of trusted relationships and a leadership style I admired. I grew under their mentorship. Around the time this leader retired, there was a broader leadership shift in the organization, and I began reporting to a new boss. He was a strong businessman, and on a personal level, I genuinely respected him.

At this same time, there was another leader in the organization (not my new boss) who I often clashed with. While they were a respected leader, we just didn't connect. And you know what? Sometimes that happens, and it doesn't mean either person is necessarily a bad person. I believe it came down to a leadership style clash. I approached HR from a perspective rooted in turning up the volume on humanity, in how we treat people and how we lead them. From my perspective, and based on how I experienced our interactions, it often felt like this leader operated at a different frequency.

Over time, that dynamic wore on me. Despite my efforts to connect, we still clashed, and the dynamic between us created tension that made it harder for me to lead my team the way I wanted to. Maybe you've experienced something similar, when no matter what you try, you just can't seem to find neutral ground with someone.

The isolation began to chip away at my confidence. It weighed on me mentally. And the hardest part was knowing others could see it: my wife, my friends, fellow leaders, and especially my HR team. If you've ever stayed in a difficult situation because you care deeply about the people depending on you, then you understand. I wanted to make it work, not just for myself, but for the team I loved leading.

The Moment that Changed Everything

Not long into this new dynamic, my boss and I met for an early morning meeting. After a brief discussion, I submitted my resignation. Bottom line: it was simply time for a change.

After I left the organization, I kept replaying the months that led up to that moment. I wondered where the distance had started, when it became too wide to cross, and why, despite everything I tried, it never came together. Even though I knew that leadership clashes like this happen, it still weighed heavily on me.

So why am I sharing this story? Here's the thing—I felt like I failed. But in reality, it wasn't failure. It was misalignment. And misalignment happens in organizations more often than we admit. Maybe you've experienced it too. And if you haven't, given enough time, you probably will. And we all process moments like that differently. Knowing it was misalignment didn't change how deeply I internalized it at the time. The decision to leave was hard, and it had a profound impact on me.

One thing that was encouraging were the texts from leaders and former coworkers who thanked me for coaching them, for helping them get promoted, for believing in them. Those words mattered more than I can explain. They reminded me that, at least for some people, I had made a difference. But here's the thing about feeling like you failed: it doesn't always let those truths sink in. The gratitude was real, but the louder voice inside me kept saying: you failed.

One night, a few weeks after I left my job, I decided that I needed to take a walk and wrestle with these feelings once and for all. For me, long walks, thinking and praying through whatever I'm facing, have always been how I decompress during tough seasons. So, around 9 p.m., I put on my shoes and told my family I was going for a walk. They were in the living room, controllers in hand, laughing and yelling at each other as they played Mario Kart. I paused in the doorway for a moment, just watching them. I kissed each of them on the forehead and said, "I love you." My son, Brooks, glanced up from the game and shouted, "I love you, Daddy!"

As I walked through the quiet streets of my neighborhood, I eventually found myself at a field I'd passed a hundred times before. I walked to the center of it and lay down on the grass, staring up at the stars. The night was clear, the air still, and for a moment it felt like the whole universe was pressing down on me.

In my heart, I was done with leadership. I was ready to quit the HR profession all together. As I looked up at the night sky I thought to myself, "where do I go from here?"

That's when my phone buzzed…it was a text from a friend.

"Hey man! Just saw the new Superman[5] movie. The scene where Lois Lane tells Superman he sees the world differently, and he says maybe that's the real punk rock, it made me think of you and all the articles you've written that you've shared with me. Dude, you're like the *PunkRocker* of HR. Stay encouraged, man. You still have work to do."

I saw the movie recently and recalled how much I loved it. If you haven't seen it, I really liked how it portrayed a different type of Superman, a more hopeful superhero who leans into his "human" imperfections. My friend even sent me a video clip of the scene. In the scene, Lois Lane is teasing Superman because he says he likes a few punk rock bands. She teases him by saying those bands are more like "Pop" groups and are terrible. He tells her he still likes them anyway:

> Lois: "My point is, I question everything. You trust everyone. You think everyone you've ever met is... beautiful."

> Superman: *"Maybe that's the real punk rock."*

Lying there in the middle of that field, it felt like those words were meant for me. My friend was right. Without realizing it, I'd been writing about and living a different style of HR, leadership, and life for years—one rooted in hope, in embracing the humanity of others, and in daring to lead differently: PunkRocker HR. And considering the leadership style clash I just had, it couldn't have been more spot

---

[5] Superman (2025) is directed and written by James Gunn. This reboot presents a more hopeful take on the Man of Steel, portraying Superman not just as an invincible hero, but as someone deeply human, kind, and optimistic in a world eager for compassion.

on. In that moment, PunkRocker HR wasn't just an idea. It was a lifeline.

As I lay there in the field, I pulled out my phone and began rereading the articles and essays I'd written over the past decade, tracing the lessons that had led me here. The chapters that follow are a journey through that night, lying in the field, revisiting the past, and realizing what *PunkRocker HR* had been all along. Each piece revealed lessons I hadn't fully seen the first time I wrote them.

So, if you're still with me, come along. Let's walk through those lessons together and see what they might stir in you, too.

Chapter 2: Hey Mr. Postman

For a long time, I just lay there in that field, the grass cool against my back, staring up at the stars. My mind was still heavy, but something inside me had shifted. I wasn't ready to stand up yet, but I was ready to start looking for something, anything, that could remind me what my purpose was as a leader.

That's when I pulled out my phone and started scrolling through the old articles and essays I'd written over the years. I hadn't read them in months. Some were for graduate school, others were just reflections I'd posted online, small attempts to make sense of leadership and life. But now, in that quiet field, they felt different, like a map leading me back to myself.

It's fitting that the first article I opened took me all the way back to where it all began — my very first career with the U.S. Postal Service. That's where I first saw what humanity in leadership really looked like, even if I didn't have the words for it yet.

The first article I reread that night was called "Hey Mr. Postman." I'd written it in 2020 for a graduate-school assignment, but the story went much further back to 1999, when I met the first HR professional who truly saw me. His name was "T." He didn't just hire me; he gave me hope. And without realizing it, he modeled what I would later come to call PunkRocker HR, leading with empathy, humor, and heart.

Begin essay:

Hey Mr. Postman

I was recently asked, "What was the first time you encountered HR in a way that made you think you might want a career in it one day?" It's a good question. In HR, it's easy to burn out or lose energy in the grind of policies, processes, and people problems. But if you go back far enough, most of us can remember a moment that planted the seed. For me, that moment came in 1999, with a gentleman I'll call "T." He was the first HR person I met who made me think, *you know what? Maybe I could do that one day.* Something he said to me that afternoon has stuck with me for 25 years, and it still drives my work today. That conversation not only introduced me to HR, but it also revealed that this field, at its best, is about something bigger than compliance or policies, it's about people, purpose, and leaving others better than you found them.

My "Loser" Phase

I graduated high school in the summer of 1998, and two of my friends and I rushed into independence by renting a three-bedroom apartment together that fall. With our low-paying, entry-level jobs, we thought we were living the American dream. But by December 1998, both my buddies had lost their jobs, we broke the lease, and I had nowhere to go.

Too embarrassed to move back home, that winter I rented the loft in a small two-bedroom house in Baltimore City owned by a friend from church named Bob. Calling it a loft is generous, it was really an attic full of boxes and cobwebs, with a small area cleared in front of a dusty window that looked out over the Baltimore skyline.

I slept on a bare twin mattress on the floor of that attic, bundled in my winter coat because the heat never made it up to the attic. Some nights I'd lie there shivering, watching my own breath as I fell asleep, wondering if this was how the rest of my life would look.

My car was a beat-up 1986 Buick Century with a rust spot the size of a pizza pan on the roof, bungee cords holding parts together, and an exhaust so loud it could've been cast in a Cheech and Chong[6] movie. By the spring of 1999, I was working as a bank teller, making minimum wage, not nearly enough for a real apartment or a reliable car. I remember being so poor, I realized that could live off five dollars a day for food by buying lunch at 7-11 (a Big Bite and Big Gulp were $2) and the dollar value menu at McDonalds ($3 for two McChicken sandwiches and a Sprite). I felt stuck. Lost. Like a loser.

My older brother was a mail carrier for the United States Postal Service in Baltimore. He made good money, had a house, a wife, kids, the whole picture of stability. The job was grueling, miles of walking in the snow, rain, or summer heat, but I wasn't afraid of hard work. I just needed a chance at more.

---

[6] Cheech & Chong films – A series of comedy movies released primarily in the 1970s and 1980s starring Richard "Cheech" Marin and Tommy Chong. The duo's movies centered on counterculture, music, and cannabis-fueled misadventures, and became cult favorites.

With my brother's encouragement, I applied to take the postal exam. Months later, I got my test date: June 1999. I prayed hard the night before, knowing this was my shot to change my life.

At the time, I had one of those alarm clocks that would play the radio station it was tuned to when it went off. My alarm clock was set to an oldies station, so when it went off the next morning to wake me up for the exam, you'll never believe what was playing on the radio...

I heard ladies singing, "Hey wait a minute Mr. Postman!" I couldn't believe my ears. It was a song titled, *"Please Mr. Postman[7]"* by The Marvelettes. When I heard those ladies singing, I thought, maybe this was a sign?

I smiled. It felt like a sign that maybe, just maybe, I was going to pass this test. Maybe things were going to work out.

Test Day

The exam was held at Bingo World, a massive auditorium in Baltimore. I'll never forget standing in line with hundreds of other people, all of us sweating in the heavy, humid summer air, waiting for the doors to open. It wasn't just hot; it was that thick Baltimore heat that makes your shirt stick to your back before the day even starts.

Eventually, they herded us inside. The room was huge, rows and rows of long tables stretching out under fluorescent lights. Each of us was handed a #2 pencil, a Scantron sheet, and a test booklet. The personnel

---

[7] "Please Mr. Postman" is a song originally recorded by The Marvelettes in 1961 and released by Motown's Tamla label. It became the first Motown song to reach No. 1 on the Billboard Hot 100.

staff running the exam looked like they would've rather been anywhere else. When they read the instructions for the exam, it was mechanical, as if they'd said the same words a thousand times before. They were sharp, rigid, almost daring anyone to raise a hand.

As soon as the test started, they began pacing the aisles, leaning over shoulders to make sure no one was cheating. The silence was so heavy you could hear the pencils scratching against paper.

I remember grinding through the questions with everything I had. This wasn't just any test; it was my shot at a different life. After about an hour, I was the first one finished. My heart was pounding as I walked my scantron sheet up to the front of the room.

The group of personnel workers sitting at the front barely looked up. One of them took my paper, glanced at it without making eye contact, and said flatly, *"If you're placed on the hiring list, someone will contact you. You may exit in the rear."*

That was it. No encouragement, no acknowledgment. Just transactional. I walked out into the heat with nothing but hope and a prayer, that I'd scored high enough to be placed on the list.

Meeting "T"

A few months later, I got the letter: I was on the hiring list! The letter invited me to an interview in November. I showed up to the Baltimore Post Office for my interview in a shirt and tie, nervous but hopeful. That's when I met "T." I didn't know it at the time, but this was my first real glimpse of what human-centered HR could look like.

T was the opposite of the Personnel "HR" folks I'd met up to that point. He was upbeat, smiling, and seemed to genuinely enjoy what he did. When he came out to get me from the lobby, he shook my hand and said, "No need to be nervous! Today is the first day of the rest of your life, young man!"

On the elevator ride up to the top floor, it was just me and him. It was very quiet, besides the moan of the elevator motor. He knew I was nervous. He leaned over quietly and said, "You know, the older I get, the less I trust stairs…"

"Really?" I asked.

"Yup," he said. "They are always… up to something!"

He looked at me and started laughing, then I laughed too. It was my first introduction to dad jokes, a love affair that continues to this day.

Inside the interview, the postmaster was stern and all business. But every time the tension spiked, "T" broke it with a joke or by calmly explaining the process. He made sure I understood what was happening. He cared.

When it ended, he walked me back to the lobby and said, *"Hang on a minute."* He disappeared into the postmaster's office, then came back a few minutes later, beaming.

"Good news," he said. "He selected you! You'll start January 1st. You'll be making $X an hour. I'll send you the official letter later today, but I can officially say it now, congratulations, Mr. Postman!"

In that moment, I heard the song again in my head: *"Wait a minute, Mr. Postman…"* And I knew my life was about to change.

I hugged him, then immediately apologized. "Sorry. I just really needed this job."

And that's when he said the words that changed me:

"No worries. That's why I get out of bed every morning to do this. Every day, I get to change lives."

With those words, and with the job he helped me secure, "T" set me on a path to a new life. I remember after starting my new job at USPS I could finally afford to trade in my broken-down car for a reliable used Honda Civic and finally get my own one-bedroom apartment. I remember the first night lying on the floor of that apartment, my own place, thanking God that I was finally on a good path. That path eventually included a 20-year career in the federal government. But more importantly, "T" showed me that HR could be more than transactional. It could be human. It could be about empathy, dignity, and hope.

That lesson still drives me today.

The Other Side of The Coin

T's approach to HR was quite a contrast to one of the first employee terminations I ever sat in on while training early in my career many years later. I was still in HR learning mode, shadowing an HR Business Partner as they walked through the process. The employee in question had struggled during their probationary period, and the decision was made to let them go. As the HR Business Partner went through the script, I noticed they skipped over the last part, the piece that explained the employee still had access to four free sessions of EAP[8] counseling, even after termination. I gently pointed it out on the script, but the HR Business Partner just shrugged me off and moved straight to asking for the employee's ID badge.

After the meeting, I asked the HR Business Partner why they chose not to mention that EAP was still available. Their response stuck with me: "The guy was a cocky jerk. I'm glad he got fired. Good riddance."

I remember thinking I didn't care if they thought he was a jerk. At the end of the day, this was a human being with a family to support. EAP counseling might have helped him process the loss of his job, cope with depression, or even realize areas where he needed to grow before his next opportunity. He at least deserved the chance to know it was there. Whether or not he chose to use it was his decision, but the HR Business Partner could have handled the termination with more heart.

Closing Thoughts

These two stories, one about "T" and one about that HR Business Partner remind me of the enormous responsibility HR carries. Getting a job and losing a job can both alter the trajectory of someone's entire life. Which means it's not enough to simply process hires and terminations "by the book." We have to do it by the "heart."

---

[8] An Employee Assistance Program (EAP) is an employer-paid benefit that provides confidential counseling and support services—often including mental health, financial, legal, and work-life resources—at no cost to employees.

When we extend a job offer, we're not just filling a role. We're giving someone a chance they've prepared for, hoped for, and maybe prayed for. That job could be the thing that helps them move out of an attic, pay off debt, or finally feel proud when their kids ask what they do for a living.

When we tell a candidate they weren't selected for a job, it's more than just sending an email or making a phone call. For them, it's the end of a hope they've been carrying through the entire interview process. How we handle that moment matters. For example, I firmly believe that if an applicant has taken the time to do a phone interview, virtual interview, or especially an in-person interview with me, and they're not chosen for the role, then they deserve at the very least a phone call. A call to thank them for their time, and to let them know we've selected another candidate. At that point, they've invested too much to only get a generic email in return. That's what it means to handle the selection process with heart, not just by the book.

When we exit someone, we're not just closing a chapter in their career. We're disrupting their routine, their confidence, and their family's sense of security. The events surrounding that decision can either add unnecessary pain, or show empathy, dignity, and respect.

At the end of the day, HR doesn't have to be transactional or rigid. Both the good moments and the hard ones can be handled with thoughtfulness that honors a person's humanity. I've always believed that nobody cares how much you know until they know how much you care. And in HR, that's the difference between managing processes and changing lives.

"T" retired not long after he hired me. But I'll never forget him, his energy, his smile, his words: *"Every day, I get to change lives."* That's the standard I try to carry forward in my own work. Because what we do in HR absolutely changes the lives of employees and families. And how we do it? That says everything about our own humanity.

End of Article

PunkRocker HR takeaway from article:

"In PunkRocker HR, we don't just process hires and exits by the book, we do it by the heart."

For me, this story captures the essence of PunkRocker HR: choosing to see people, not just processes. As I reread this article while lying in that field, I thought about how easily we overlook the human side of work, especially when someone resigns or is terminated. Many companies have an Employee Assistance Program (EAP) that offers free counseling for employees who may need support as they navigate big transitions. Whenever someone leaves, whether by choice or not, I always make sure they know about that benefit and how long they can still use it. Employees pour so much of their mental and emotional energy into an organization; the least we can do is look out for their well-being as they exit.

"T" wasn't just filling a spot on a roster. He gave dignity, hope, and confidence to someone who badly needed it. That's rebellion in a world where HR often hides behind forms and procedures. Have you ever had someone like that in your life, a leader, mentor, or even a coworker, who saw something in you that you couldn't yet see in yourself? Those are the people who change us.

The contrast couldn't be sharper: one leader showed up with kindness that lifted someone up; another chose to look past someone's humanity in one of the hardest moments of their life. That's the core of PunkRocker HR: remembering that every hire, rejection, and exit isn't just paperwork—it's a moment that can shape the course of someone's life. When we handle those moments with heart, not just by the book, we don't just "do HR." We make a difference in a human being's life.

In that field, rereading this story reminded me that the best leaders aren't always the loudest; they're the ones who show up with quiet humanity, even when no one's watching.

Call to Action:

Are you leading with the heart in your hires and exits, or just following the book?

Chapter 3: Calm in the Storm

The next article I reread that night was titled "Calm in the Storm." I'd written it while leading a mentoring program as an HR Leader, but the story itself took me back twenty years, to a moment that changed everything. It's a story I don't share often because it's deeply personal, but I include it here for one reason: it shows how powerful mentorship can be. What began as one supervisor's quiet example became a defining mindset, one that still shapes how I lead, work, and live.

Begin Article:

The Calm in the Storm

The other night, my wife and I were watching one of my favorite shows, *Modern Family*[9]. The show follows a father, his grown children, and their families as they navigate the chaos of everyday life in "modern" society. One character, Phil Dunphy, is married to Claire, and their relationship always cracks me up. Phil means well, but his antics usually frustrate Claire, which makes their arguments hilarious to watch.

One scene stuck with me. Phil and Claire are sitting on the couch, being interviewed. Claire is wound up, venting about how maddening

---

[9] Modern Family – An American television sitcom that aired on ABC from 2009 to 2020. The show follows the lives of the Pritchett-Dunphy-Tucker family in a mockumentary style, starring Ed O'Neill, Julie Bowen, Ty Burrell, Sofia Vergara, and others. It became a critical and commercial success, winning 22 Primetime Emmy Awards, including five for Outstanding Comedy Series.

it is that Phil stays calm under pressure. Without missing a beat, Phil leans in and says gently, *"That's it, let it all out."* Claire glares at him, her voice dripping with sarcasm as she mutters, *"I am going to kill you."*

It's a funny moment, but it captures something I've come to believe is critical for HR: being the calm in the storm. For some, like Phil, it seems natural. For others, it's a muscle that only builds after years of practice. Either way, in HR, where people bring you their storms daily, having the ability to steady the ship is one of the most powerful tools you can have.

After the episode, my wife turned to me and said, "Oh my God. You are just like Phil Dunphy. Your calmness when I get upset drives me crazy. How did you get to be this way?"

I laughed, but the question stuck. How *did* I get this way? My mind drifted back to my time at USPS in Baltimore, to an afternoon I hadn't thought about in years.

Learning Calm the Hard Way

Being a mail carrier in Baltimore was no joke. The routes could stretch for miles, through rowhouse blocks in the blazing heat or freezing rain. Your legs burned and your shoulders ached from the satchel carrying the weight of packages and mail.

I was part of a new class of young carriers in the early 2000s, and it wasn't uncommon to hear others grumble about the routes. As the junior employees, we usually got the leftovers—the routes nobody wanted. Some days it felt like punishment, trudging up endless staircases or battling dogs that seemed to take guarding the mailbox as a sacred duty.

But then there was "M." My first supervisor. M had this presence about him, steady, collected, unshakable. When tempers flared, when deliveries backed up, when chaos seemed to win, M never lost his cool. He didn't raise his voice. He didn't match fire with fire. He steadied the moment.

I admired that, and without realizing it, I began imitating him. Anytime the work felt overwhelming, I'd whisper to myself: *"Be the calm in the storm. Just like M."*

And then came the day that lesson became more than words.

It was the fall of 2001. I had just turned 21. The air was unseasonably warm, heavy in that sticky way that makes Baltimore heat feels like an outdoor sauna. My shirt was damp, my satchel cutting into my shoulder as I finished what felt like the hundredth block of the day. Around 5 p.m., I pulled my truck onto the last street. "Just one more stretch," I told myself.

I swung open the back door of the truck and leaned in, grabbing the last few packages. That's when I heard it.

"Hey..." a deep voice said from behind me.

I turned, and my stomach dropped. A young man who appeared to be in his late teens stood there in a dark blue hoodie, his hand gripping a gun leveled straight at me. I had no idea if the gun was real or not, but in those moments, you don't ask.

For a split second, panic surged. My heart hammered so hard it felt like it might burst. "I thought, 'This is it.'" But then M's voice filled my head: *"Be the calm in the storm,"* I told myself.

"Give me what you got," he demanded, motioning at the packages with his free hand.

I moved slowly, deliberately. No sudden movements. I picked up three boxes, extended them toward him, and then raised my hands high.

He grabbed the packages and turned to run. Relief rushed in. "Thank God, it's over," I thought.

But it wasn't.

After a few steps, he stopped. His shoulders tightened, and he slowly turned back toward me. Our eyes met. He raised the gun again, this time aiming for my chest. I realized what he must have been thinking: no mask, no disguise. He thought I could identify him.

Time slowed to a crawl. I could hear my breath, ragged and uneven. I could feel the sweat running down my back. I closed my eyes and braced.

Click.

The gun misfired.

He cursed under his breath, pulled the trigger again.

Click.

Another misfire.

He yanked the trigger again; his face twisted with frustration.

Click.

Three misfires. Three bullets that should have ended me.

Then, with a final string of curses, he turned and bolted. His footsteps pounded the pavement until they faded into silence.

I stood frozen, my arms still raised, the sound of those clicks echoing in my ears. My knees nearly buckled as I sat down hard on the bumper of my truck. I was alive. Somehow, I was alive.

The Lesson from my Mentor

Back at the post office, I told M what had happened. We called the police, filed the report, gave a description. Nothing ever came of it.

But I'll never forget what M said afterward. He leaned back in his chair, studied me for a moment, and said, "From the way you described it, you stayed calm. That's rare. It'll serve you well in life."

I looked at him and said quietly, "If I was calm, it's only because I learned it by watching you. Thank you for showing me how to be the calm in the storm."

Even now, more than twenty years later, I know how close I came. By all rights, I should have died that day. I shouldn't have met my wife five years later. I shouldn't have held my kids for the first time or been here writing this story. But I believe that the lesson I learned from M, being the calm in the storm, helped save my life.

Being the calm in the storm continues to save me, over and over again, in boardrooms, in HR offices, and in moments of chaos that don't make the news but feel just as heavy to the people going through them.

For leaders, for HR professionals, for anyone who finds themselves in the middle of the storm: learn calm. Practice it. Because when the storm comes, and it will, people will look to you. And your calm may just change everything, and perhaps even save lives.

End of Article

PunkRocker HR takeaway from article:

In PunkRocker HR, we are the calm in the storm.

As I read that article again that night, lying in the field, here's what stood out to me: Workplaces can run on chaos, deadlines, crises, and constant urgency. Maybe you've felt it too, that moment when everything around you is spinning, and you're trying to decide whether to react or respond.

Being calm doesn't mean you're passive or fearless. It means you're choosing not to let fear or frustration take over. In HR, calm shows up in those quiet, critical moments, when you steady an employee in crisis, de-escalate a heated conversation, or help a leader navigate uncertainty.

Calm isn't just a personality trait; it's a responsibility. Sometimes, it's the one thing that keeps a situation, or a person, from breaking.

Call to Action:

When the storm hits your workplace, are you adding to the noise or choosing to be the calm that others can hold onto?

Chapter 4: The Holidays and a Special Delivery

As I continued to read in that field, I stood up and stretched my legs. I looked up at the moon, which was now visible, and I appreciated the extra light to help me read on. The next article I read, I wrote just before Christmas in 2021. I found myself reflecting on how precious time really is during the holidays, and a recent interaction brought that truth home to me in a powerful way.

My hope in writing it was to remind both leaders and employees to pause, to value the time they have with the people who love them most. It's easy to forget that we're more than our titles or deadlines. The people who love us most don't measure us by our productivity; they love us unconditionally. And it's in those moments with them that we discover our greatest wealth.

Begin Article:

The Holidays and a Special Delivery

Growing up, Christmastime was my favorite time of the year. I loved the lights, the weather, the build-up to that one special day. I have many younger sisters, so as a big brother, I loved seeing each one of them come down the stairs on Christmas morning, their eyes lighting up when they saw their gifts under the tree. I loved sipping eggnog and getting yelled at by my mom as my dad and I ate half the cookie dough before she could bake the cookies. I can still feel my mom's wooden spoon smacking me on the back of the head.

I also loved the trek across the Chesapeake Bay Bridge to see my grandparents on the Eastern Shore of Maryland every Christmas Eve for our family party. When I was young, I didn't realize the value of the memories I was building until I became a parent myself.

Recently, my 7-year-old son, Brooks, asked me what the greatest Christmas gift I ever received was. I had to think about it. Was it the PlayStation I got in high school? No, it had to be something else. Maybe it was the Baltimore Ravens Ray Lewis jersey I got during my senior year of high school. Not that either. As I thought about it, a memory suddenly came to mind.

A Christmas Delivery

I remembered back when I was first hired by the U.S. Postal Service at the age of 18 as a mail carrier. That first year was a tough one. I was a "PTF" letter carrier, what they called those of us who hadn't yet earned a full-time route. I was in an office filled with retired U.S. Marines and Army reservists. These men and women did their best to break me in and show me the ropes. They were tough on me, but they helped me grow up quickly.

Fast forward to Christmas 2001. I was 21 years old. Back then, the junior carrier was assigned to come in on Christmas Day around 8 a.m. and deliver whatever priority or express packages came in that morning, generally about a two-hour shift. I was single, no wife or kids, so I gladly took the shift. I wore a Santa hat just for fun when delivering the packages.

I still remember what it was like to deliver those boxes: people opening their doors with kids tearing into presents in the background.

It made me look forward to the day I could experience that with my own family.

As I was leaving that day, I noticed a strange box on one of the carrier's cases. It had an APO return address. The delivery address was badly scuffed and hard to read, which is why it was probably destined to be returned to sender. But I thought of one address it could be. I could've left it there, but something told me to grab it and give it a try. So, I did. I punched out and went to deliver it on my way home.

I knocked on the door of the house, and an older lady answered. I explained that the address was scuffed but asked if she was expecting a package from an APO. I showed her the box, and she started crying and hugged me. Inside the house, I saw two young children.

Turns out, the package was from her daughter, a service member deployed after 9/11. The box held gifts for her kids. The woman I handed the package to was the children's grandmother. She cried because she didn't think the package would arrive on time, or at all. She thanked me over and over and even gave me a glass of eggnog for my troubles (nonalcoholic ... or so she said with a wink).

Eventually, that house ended up on my first permanent route for about five years. I got to know those grandparents well before moving on to other routes and eventually into management with the Postal Service. When it rained, they'd let me hang out on their porch.

I remember another time when I delivered a large package to their house several months later. As I squatted down to set it inside their door, I heard a loud tear. My mailman shorts ripped clean down my backside, leaving a gaping hole (yes, this really happens). While this new "vent" in my shorts provided a nice breeze on a hot day, I couldn't help feel a bit embarrassed. The grandmother saw, laughed hysterically, then handed me a pair of her son's blue basketball shorts so I could finish my route that day.

Time, Not Things

Fast forward nearly 20 years. I had since retired from the post office and moved on. One day in February 2020, I was at the Arundel Mills Mall with my kids, eating at the food court. An older woman tapped me on the shoulder; it was that same grandmother. She had recognized me.

We caught up for a few moments, and standing beside her was her daughter, the service member whose package I had delivered all those years ago. It was the first time I had met her in person. She thanked me and showed me a picture of her sons, now grown men in U.S. Army uniforms. That was awesome.

I told her I'd left the post office and now worked in HR at a community college, a move that let me spend more time with my family. Before she walked away, she said something I'll never forget:

"You know what I've learned? My husband passed away 10 years ago. I've seen the world change. But one thing has never changed: the most precious commodity in life is time. Not money, not your job, not cars or houses. Time. Nobody on their deathbed ever wishes for more money or things. They always wish for more time."

She hugged me and walked away. That was one of the most profound conversations of my life. I guess I'd always known the value of time, especially at Christmas. But that day, it hit home in a way I'll never forget.

The Greatest Gift

Fast forward to Thanksgiving 2021. I got a Facebook message from her daughter: her mom had passed away peacefully in her sleep at age 80, the day after Thanksgiving. She told me her mother's last day was spent doing what she loved most, spending time with her family. I'd say she left this earth a wealthy woman, having invested in the greatest commodity of all right up to the end.

Thank you, Mrs. Ruth, for the wisdom, and for the spare pair of blue shorts on that fateful day.

As this memory came back to me, I turned to Brooks and told him the greatest Christmas gift is the time I get to spend with my family every year. He hugged me, looked up, and said, "Yeah, but Daddy, if I got a Nintendo Switch this year, that would be pretty cool."

For a second, I thought he'd completely missed my point.

"Getting a Nintendo Switch is better than spending time with your family?" I asked.

He replied, "No! I want one so we can all spend time together and play every day!"

Well... maybe he got the point after all. Or maybe it was just his sales pitch for Santa. Either way, well played, son.

John Lennon once said, *"Life is what happens when you're busy making other plans."* The holiday season is no different. We all get busy chasing the perfect gift, but life is short, and our time is limited.

This holiday season, whatever you celebrate, remember, it's not about the gifts under the tree. It's about the time we spend with the ones we love. That's what lasts.

More valuable than silver or gold. More valuable than an extra pair of shorts when your pair rips down the rear. More valuable than even a Nintendo Switch.

Time is the greatest gift we'll ever have. And for me, a special Christmas delivery nearly 20 years ago will always remind me of that.

Happy Holidays!

End of Article

PunkRocker HR takeaway from article:

"In PunkRocker HR, we honor time as the greatest gift, especially the time employees spend with their families."

PunkRocker HR doesn't just write work-life balance into a handbook: it lives it. We know an employee's time with their family is more important than their time with us. Our job as leaders is to protect that balance, not chip away at it.

Have you ever felt that too? That nagging sense that you're giving too much time to the wrong things, while the moments that really matter keep slipping away?

That's why we have to be intentional. It means respecting boundaries, encouraging people to unplug, and building workplaces where no one's expected to trade their best years for a paycheck.

Because here's the truth: at the end of the day, people don't remember the late nights or the extra emails. They remember dinner around the table, holidays with their kids, laughter with friends.

That's why PunkRocker HR treats time as sacred, because it's the most valuable thing we have. Honoring it is one of the clearest ways to prove we truly care.

As I sat there in that field, the moonlight fading behind the clouds, I thought about Mrs. Ruth's words: time is the greatest gift. She was right. Because when we finally slow down long enough to appreciate time, we start to notice something else that's just as powerful: the people who fill it.

Call to Action:

Do your employees believe you genuinely value all of their time, or just the time they give to work?

Chapter 5: The Silver Lining

A few drops of rain began to fall as I read the next article. Not enough to send me running for cover, just enough to cool the air. I wasn't ready to move yet. The next piece was one I'd written in April 2020, right after leaving a 20-year career with the Postal Service to start a new HR role in another organization. Then the world stopped. COVID hit. Overnight, everything changed.

At the time, I felt anxious, uncertain, and frustrated—about my work, my family, and the future. But looking back now, I see what I couldn't then: that I was already practicing one of the quietest PunkRocker HR traits, learning to look for the silver linings when everything feels upside down.

Begin Article:

The Silver Lining

There I was, sitting on the couch in my living room, getting frustrated. As part of the new normal during the COVID-19 pandemic, I was trying to log into our weekly Zoom staff meeting. As I was furiously trying to log in, I got the spinning wheel of death on my computer screen, and the application would not let me into the meeting. I kept refreshing over and over again and still, no entry. Sitting next to me on my couch was my 8-year-old daughter, Zoey. She was getting frustrated, trying to log into her Google Classroom, begging me for help with tears in her eyes. I was trying to help her and help myself, then I heard a shout from my 5-year-old son Brooks from the bathroom:

"Daddy, I flushed the potty, but the water is still coming out all over the floor!"

My wife was at work, and I was losing my cool. I was frustrated with so many things. First, there was the ongoing pandemic and the shutdown of so much of our lives. There were friends who had either been infected or lost loved ones to this tragic virus, who I had been praying for. There were also many friends and family who had lost their jobs. Then there was the anxiety of my own job security. Schools were being shut down as parents tried to teach their kids from home. It was like a volcano was building up and frustration finally erupted inside of me. Then it happened. I shouted, "Oh my God... this sucks!"

My children were both shocked. I never raise my voice. In fact, my wife says arguing with me is like arguing with Mr. Bean[10]. My daughter immediately took offense and ran to her room. My son came running out of the bathroom, with his pants around his ankles asking, "What sucks, Daddy? Is it me?"

I tried to speak. I tried to say something to cover my error, but he slowly turned around in sadness, walking toward his bedroom with a six-foot piece of toilet paper stuck to his foot, trailing behind him. I was embarrassed for shouting those words, and I knew it affected my kids that day.

I sat back, looked up at the ceiling, and breathed in deeply. "You're an idiot, John!" I thought to myself. I slowly got up and began to clean

---

[10] Mr. Bean is a British comedy character created and portrayed by Rowan Atkinson. The character, known for his near-total silence and exaggerated physical humor, first appeared on television in 1990.

the disaster that was our bathroom. Realizing I was going to need our dehumidifier, I went to the basement storage room and began to search. I bumped into the wall, and something fell from a top shelf and struck me in the head. It was a dusty old piece of sports memorabilia from an Orioles game 25 years ago. I picked it up, stared at it, and memories of the day I got it suddenly came back to me. It was then that I began to realize a piece of advice given to me that day by my father, long forgotten in the midst of the stresses of my current life and the pandemic.

Give That Fan a Contract

It was June 1995. I was fourteen years old, at Camden Yards with my dad. He wasn't an overly affectionate man, a loveable combination of Archie Bunker[11] and Tim "The Tool Man" Taylor[12]. However, baseball was how we connected. Sitting there with a beer in his hand and peanut shells at his feet, he actually looked happy. I remember staring at his beat-up hands, scarred from decades as a mechanic and small business owner.

He caught me looking and said, "I'm sorry I missed so many of your baseball games. Running a business takes more than I ever imagined. I wish I could be home more."

---

[11] Archie Bunker – A fictional character from the classic American sitcom All in the Family (1971–1979). Played by Carroll O'Connor, Archie was a working-class man known for his blunt, often prejudiced views, which the show used to tackle social and political issues with humor and tension.
[12] Tim the Tool Man" Taylor – The main character from the sitcom Home Improvement (1991–1999), played by comedian Tim Allen. Tim Taylor was the accident-prone host of a DIY home repair TV show, known for his grunts, catchphrases, and well-meaning but often disastrous attempts at fixing things.

I asked him, "Is it worth it? Missing so much just for work?"

He patted my shoulder and gave me advice I'd forgotten for 25 years:

"Sometimes, you have to look for the silver linings. Life moves fast. Seize the small moments. Be thankful for them. Those are what you'll remember."

Not long after, a foul ball came screaming our way. I stuck out my glove and snagged it clean. The PA announcer boomed, "Give that fan a contract!" and within minutes, ushers came by to gather my contact information. Then, a few weeks later, in the mail came an "honorary off-field fielder" contract from the Baltimore Orioles. I eventually got this "contract" framed, which over the years hung on my wall and became that dusty piece of sports memorabilia that would fall and hit me in the head. For years, I told that story as a funny memory about catching a ball and getting a contract. But the real gift of that day wasn't the foul ball, it was my dad's words about silver linings, words I wouldn't truly understand until much later.

This is Actually Awesome

Back to the present day, I looked at my laptop and work in front of me. It suddenly dawned on me that I was the same age my dad was that day at the Orioles game: 39 years old. I completed my Zoom meeting, then I closed my laptop. I thought about the last four years of my life. I spent weeks on business travel for the federal government, traveling the country conducting trainings. During those years, living out of a suitcase, I missed a lot of my kids' events. I missed school plays, dinners, and reading books before bedtime on numerous occasions. I missed a lot of the "small things" for work. Early in 2020,

I retired from federal service to take a job at my local community college to be closer to home and have a better work-life balance. Then the pandemic hit, and suddenly I got a lot of "home" in my work-life balance.

The problem was, I had gotten so frustrated with the difficulty of working from home, helping my kids do schoolwork, and the anxiety over the future, that I failed to see the "silver lining." First, I was blessed to even still have a job and work remotely. Also, I was finally getting the time with my kids that I never got over the past four years. I got to see them wake up every day. I got to eat breakfast and lunch with them. If I wanted to take a little break, I could read a book with them. I could go for a walk with them or play outside with them (since I was now home while the sun was still up). I was getting to make up for four years of being gone. Instead of yelling "Oh my God... this sucks," I should have yelled, "Oh my God, this... this is awesome."

I understand that perspective is important. There is a lot of pain in the world. Many have tragically lost loved ones to the COVID-19 virus. Many have lost jobs, livelihoods, and their 401k's are nearly gone. Friendships have been strained, etc. My revelation here about the "silver lining" isn't meant to minimize any of that. The tragedy is real and heartbreaking.

Whatever your situation is, during the stress and anxiety of this pandemic, I would encourage you to pause for a moment. Take a deep breath and think, "What is the silver lining in all of this?" What small things have you been able to do right now that you couldn't do before? What have you learned about yourself, your family, or coworkers that has strengthened your relationships? What skills have you refined under pressure during this time that have made you a better professional, leader, parent, or friend? Is there a roof over your head, food on the table, and Netflix to binge with a loved one? There is good reason to be concerned with the big, heavy things. However, take a moment to be thankful for the small things. There you will find your silver lining, and hopefully some peace.

As I sat there after my Zoom meeting, I began to think about what life would be like for my children 25 years from now. Chances are they will probably be where I am, immersed in their work, kids, bills, and who knows what pandemic may even be taking place at that time. How would they know to remember to look for the silver lining? How could I set an example?

Then I remembered the basement, and that old piece of sports memorabilia. For years, this contract hung on the wall everywhere I lived and served as a great conversation piece. I would always tell the story of how I caught the ball but always seemed to forget to mention my dad's advice prior to the foul ball. In retrospect, his advice was worth so much more than an honorary contract and a ball. In fact, the time I spent with him at that game was just as valuable. I just didn't realize it until now.

I realized I had taken it off the wall a few years back when we were doing some painting and totally forgot to put it back up. There it sat for years, gathering dust for the right moment to fall and smack me in the head. To be honest, I deserved a smack in the head. I went back to the basement, grabbed the plaque with the contract and ball, cleaned it up and gave it to my son, Brooks.

He looked up and asked, "Daddy, why did you give this to me?"

I said, "Because one day you'll need to remember to look for the silver linings too."

"Silver linings? What are those?" he asked.

"Tell you what," I said, "when you're in your late 30's with a wife, kids, and a job, I'll tell you all about it over a cold beer."

"I like root beer too, Daddy!" Brooks said.

I laughed for the first time in a few days when he said that. Then together, we hung the contract on the wall of his bedroom, and he was so excited to have it there. I turned to both of my kids and apologized for my "outburst" earlier. They both hugged me. At that moment, I realized I forgot to finish cleaning the bathroom disaster…

After fixing the bathroom massacre my son had left me, my daughter came up to me and grabbed my hand. She said, "Do you want to go play some whiffle ball in the front yard with our friends?"

I looked out my son's bedroom window and saw a handful of kids, aged 5–10, with a whiffle ball bat and ball, waving for us to come outside. It was like a scene from the movie *The Sandlot*[13]. I looked over at my laptop and my work as it lay on the table. I knew I had a lot of work to do. But then I remembered my father's words, "Be thankful for the few and small moments. Those are the silver linings you'll

---

[13] The Sandlot – A coming-of-age sports comedy film released in 1993, directed by David Mickey Evans. Set in the summer of 1962, it follows a young boy and his neighborhood friends bonding over baseball, adventures, and childhood mischief, making it a nostalgic favorite about friendship and growing up.

remember for the rest of your life." I decided to take an early lunch break.

I looked back at my children and said, "Absolutely."

Together, we played a game of whiffle ball with their friends. I had not played whiffle ball in years, and it showed as I embarrassed myself. As I ran the bases made from frisbees, I realized I may have eaten one too many Chick-fil-A milkshakes during the pandemic shutdown. But at that moment, I completely forgot there was a pandemic. I completely forgot about the anxiety of my job security, school closings, and wearing masks at stores. For a moment, I was one of the kids again. Just as I did with my dad at that Orioles game so many years ago, I relished the sounds of the crowd, the crack of the (plastic) bat, and the spring sun shining on our faces. For a moment, life seemed normal.

I must confess I shouted out loud again. But this time the words were different, as I shouted, "Oh my God, this... this is awesome."

My friends, especially during these times, always look for the silver linings in life.

End of Article

PunkRocker HR takeaway from article:

In PunkRocker HR, we look for the silver linings.

Not the forced kind, or the "think positive" stuff that ignores what hurts, but the quiet kind that shows up when life gives you every reason to give up. Gratitude that's real, not performative.

Have you ever felt that too, that pull to let frustration or burnout win, only to catch a small moment that reminded you why you still care?

That's what PunkRocker HR is about. It's choosing gratitude when it's not easy. It's finding the small flashes of good, the laughter that sneaks in, the person who shows up for you, the reason you keep showing up for others.

Silver linings don't erase the pain; they anchor us in purpose. In HR, that means helping people find perspective and dignity, even when we can't fix the storm around them. That's the heart of this work, and the heart of PunkRocker HR.

Call to Action:

When challenges show up, do you pause long enough to notice the silver linings that could give you, and those around you, the strength to keep going?

Chapter 6: Hope is a Good Thing

The rain had stopped, but the air was heavy. I still wanted to keep reading. I opened the next article, one I'd written in the summer of 2020, right in the heart of the COVID pandemic, during my time in higher education HR.

Everywhere I looked back then, coworkers, students, even my own kids, people were worn down by hopelessness. The question on everyone's mind was, "When will this end?" As HR professionals, we weren't just managing policies or Zoom calls; we were carrying the emotional weight of people trying to hold their lives together.

Looking back, I see now that what kept me moving, and what I tried to give others, was one of the most PunkRocker HR truths of all: when hope starts to fade, you fight to keep it alive.

Begin Article:

Hope is a Good Thing

One of the highlights of my life was July 4, 2011. There I sat in our hospital room at St. Agnes Hospital, holding my brand-new baby girl, Zoey. I looked out the window, and in the distance, I could see fireworks bursting in the sky over the Inner Harbor of Baltimore. It was one of those awe-inspiring moments where you know, even as you're living it, that it will stay with you forever. Not once did Zoey cry during the fireworks, but she squeezed my hand each time one exploded. I was a nervous new father, but in those tiny squeezes I felt a wave of hope for what the future might bring for us.

At the end of the fireworks, I could tell it was time for a diaper change. That's when I said to my wife, "I think Zoey wants you," and ran like heck to the cafeteria for a snack…

Fast forward nine years later, and watching fireworks on Zoey's birthday had become a yearly family tradition. But this year would be different. Due to the COVID-19 pandemic, most fireworks celebrations in our area were canceled. When I told Zoey, she was sad but understood the reasons why. Still, I couldn't help but notice the look on her face, a look of hopelessness, like yet another piece of life worth looking forward to had been taken away. School was closed, playgrounds were closed, movie theaters were closed, and so many other joys were canceled, paused, or kept at a distance. She wasn't the only one. I felt it too. Have you ever felt that way? Like the light had gone out a little, and you weren't sure how to get it back?

It's heartbreaking to see the loss of hope in a loved one. And in 2020, hopelessness seemed to be the theme of the year. Turn on the TV, and you saw and anger everywhere. Underneath it all, I saw a lack of hope. People had lost jobs. Paychecks stopped coming. Protesters marched because they saw no justice to look forward to. These weren't just stories, they were real lives, and the ripple effects touched us all.

Still, deep down, I hoped to find some way to make Zoey's birthday special.

Hope is a Dangerous Thing

One night, as I was trying to figure out a way to make Zoey's birthday special, I was flipping through channels on the TV. I came across *The*

Shawshank Redemption[14]. I hadn't seen it in over 14 years, but this time a theme stood out that I had missed before: hope.

If you've never seen it, Andy Dufresne is a man wrongfully imprisoned for the murder of his wife and her lover. Throughout the movie, he clings to hope that one day he'll be free. In one powerful scene near the end, Andy tries to explain the importance of hope to his friend Red, who pushes back: *"Hope is a dangerous thing."*

Is hope dangerous? Hope is defined as "a feeling of expectation and desire for a certain thing to happen." And yet, the most heartbreaking thing I saw that year wasn't just the loss of hope across our country, it was the loss of hope in my own daughter's eyes. I realized I had forgotten how powerful hope really is — that hope for the future, for better days ahead, is what keeps life exciting and worth moving forward. Have you ever needed to be reminded of that, too?

Just as I was finishing the movie, I heard a crash from the den. A ball had been launched inside the house by one of my kids, shattering the frame around one of my favorite pictures — a poster of Cole Field House, where the Maryland Terrapins used to play. The picture itself was fine, but that frame had history. It was the first frame I ever bought for my first house.

---

[14] The Shawshank Redemption – A 1994 drama film directed by Frank Darabont, based on Stephen King's novella. It tells the story of Andy Dufresne, a banker wrongly imprisoned for murder, and his decades-long friendship with fellow inmate Red, exploring themes of hope, resilience, and redemption.

As I knelt to pick up the pieces, my kids noticed the look on my face.

"What's wrong, Daddy?" Zoey asked. "Sorry we broke the frame. Are we in trouble?"

"No," I said. "It was an accident. It's just that this picture frame has a special memory behind it."

"What's so special about a poster frame?" Zoey asked. "Will you tell us?"

"Sure," I said, smiling. "The story of that frame starts with a journey, one that led to an encounter I'll never forget."

Lose the Zero and Get with the Hero

The story behind how I purchased the frame is life changing. I remember it like it was yesterday. The date was March 17, 2005. I had just bought a townhome in Columbia, Maryland. The walls were bare except for that Terps poster, which I had literally tacked to the wall. My younger sisters mocked me for it, along with the fact that the only things in my refrigerator were Hot Pockets, Top Ramen, and Capri Suns, a typical single guy diet. Finally, they wore me down and told me I needed to go to a store and buy an actual frame for the Terps poster. The next day on my way home from work, I took their advice.

So, there I was, 25 years old, still in my U.S. Postal Service uniform, wandering clueless through a Michaels Arts and Crafts store when I spotted a frame that looked about right. As I walked up to the register, I noticed a beautiful young woman standing near the cashier. She smiled at me, then disappeared into the manager's office.

The cashier leaned in and said, "Hey man, that was my supervisor. She thinks you're cute. You should go ask for her number."

Normally I had a rule: don't bother someone at work like that. But this felt like a sign. So, I walked nervously to the manager's office and knocked on the door. The young lady came out, and we chatted for a few minutes about picture frames (real smooth, I know). She was kind, funny, and gorgeous. Finally, I asked if she'd like to grab a coffee sometime.

She smiled and said, "I'm so sorry, I would, but I'm seeing someone." Then she rolled her eyes and added, "He was supposed to pick me up from work ten minutes ago, but he's late again, as usual."

That's when something snapped. Out came the cheesiest line I've ever used in my life:

> "Well, since he's always late, maybe you should…

> … ditch the Zero and get with the Hero."

And yes, I actually pointed to myself.

The second it left my mouth, I regretted it. But then she laughed. *"You're funny!"* she said. She then scribbled her number on a piece of paper and handed it to me. "Maybe we can grab coffee as friends."

I left the store, and a few days had passed but I hadn't called that girl just yet. A few days later, I told my stepmom the story. However, she didn't laugh. I told her that I **hoped** I eventually would get a chance to take her out on a date. My Stepmom said, "Hope is great, but what good is hope without action? She gave you her number for a reason. You should call her."

I didn't call right away. But eventually, I did.

And after a first date followed by a year and a half of several more, eventually, in 2006, I married that girl from the frame shop.

Turns out, hope plus action works.

I Never Lost My Hope in You

Back to the present day, I thought about this concept of hope in action. I knew I had to try to make fireworks happen for Zoey's birthday. Through a family contact, I found out about a small public display still happening on July 4. We made the drive.

Zoey's face was worried at first, like she didn't want to get her hopes up. But when the first fireworks lit the sky, she grabbed my hand, just like she did as a baby nine years earlier. This time, though, her eyes filled with tears of joy.

"Thank you, Daddy," she said softly. "I knew you'd find a way."

"How did you know?" I asked.

"Because I never lost my hope in you. You're my hero."

I'd never been called a hero before, and I wasn't sure I deserved it. But to her, I did. In that moment, I understood something: hope isn't just about what we look forward to — it's about the trust we place in each other.

As I stood in that field, fireworks exploding overhead, I realized I'd spent too many moments in life feeling like the "Zero." But right there, surrounded by my wife, my son, and my daughter who believed in me, I felt like a "Hero."

Whatever you're going through right now, it's okay to feel the sting of disappointment. But never, ever lose hope.

Because chances are, there's someone out there who has never lost their hope in you.

End of Article

PunkRocker HR takeaway from article:

Hope is human. In PunkRocker HR, we fight to keep it alive.

Hope isn't just optimism, it's survival. People come to us in moments of fear and uncertainty, when the path forward isn't clear. And sometimes, the most powerful thing we can offer isn't an answer, but a reason to believe that tomorrow can still be better.

Have you ever felt that too? That moment when someone's counting on you, and you don't have the fix, but you can still offer presence, faith, and hope?

Sympathy says, "I feel bad for you."

Empathy says, "I'm here with you."

PunkRocker HR chooses empathy every time. We meet people where they are, carry a bit of their weight, and help them find their footing again. Because when we help someone hold onto hope, we're not just doing HR, we're restoring humanity.

Call to Action:

When the people around you are struggling, do you just offer sympathy from a distance, or are you willing to stand with them in their hurt and help them hold onto hope?

Chapter 7: Authentic Appreciation

The night was quiet again, and for the first time, I could feel a little hope stirring, but I wasn't there yet. The next article I opened was from February 2021, written during my time in higher education HR. I had originally written it to kick off Employee Appreciation Day, tying appreciation to business results. But reading it now, I see it was about something deeper, one of the truest PunkRocker HR lessons of all: that authentic appreciation isn't a perk or a slogan. It's how leaders build real connection, and real results, one thank-you at a time.

Begin Article:

Employee Appreciation? That's No Big Deal.

I still remember the day I heard that statement. It was January 2007, and I was in the U.S. Postal Service's operations supervisor training program. It was a required training program that combined classroom and on-the-job training to prepare us for leadership. In my class, there was a fellow trainee I will never forget. He was incredibly smart and talented. He understood the operation manuals, collective bargaining agreements, Key Performance Indicators (KPIs), and everything else better than I did. I was in awe of his expertise. He'd already served as an interim supervisor several times before the program even started.

Toward the end of the program, one of our last workshops was on the topic of employee engagement. When the speaker began talking about employee appreciation, my fellow trainee rolled his eyes and said, "Employee appreciation? That's no big deal. All that matters in the end is meeting your KPIs." Then he left the room for a break and didn't return until the next seminar. I was shocked. But I'll tell you more about his story in a moment.

Was my fellow supervisor trainee right or wrong? Does employee appreciation really matter and have a measurable benefit? Some people say (and I've heard it personally) that employee appreciation is just "fluffy HR talk" meant to get you to be nice to your employees. Have you ever heard that too? Or maybe even thought it yourself at one point? The truth is, recognition and appreciation are both vital parts of engagement, but they're not the same thing. Employee recognition spotlights great work toward a goal or objective. Employee appreciation spotlights how the employee is valued overall. In simple terms: recognition is about what people do; appreciation is about who they are.

And yes, appreciation really does make a difference, not just for morale, but for performance, trust, and retention. People stay where they feel seen. When they know they matter, they don't just do the work, they care about the work.

Some of the benefits of regular employee appreciation include enhanced motivation, increased morale, a sense of accomplishment, stronger engagement, and higher productivity. Considering these benefits, what are some ways you can show appreciation on a regular basis?

- **Say thank you.** It sounds simple, but it matters. An employee once told me that in their regular one-on-one meetings, their manager always took a moment to thank them for their work. That small gesture made the employee feel valued—and motivated them even more.

- **Remember the small stuff.** Birthdays, anniversaries (work or otherwise), and special achievements matter. If someone completes a special assignment, celebrate it publicly with the team.
- **Have fun and be creative.** Send a handwritten thank-you card. Create funny awards. A former HR manager I worked with gave out spontaneous trophies—even for silly things like "best hair in the office" (spoiler: my hair situation is more Bruce Willis than Brad Pitt). One employee got a trophy for "best shoes in the office" because she loved shopping and had a massive collection. Creativity shows authenticity.
- **Ask for input.** Give employees a chance to share ideas or feedback. Simply asking, "What do you think?" shows you value their voice.
- **Shine a light on the unsung heroes.** Some employees do incredible work behind the scenes and rarely get recognized. Give them an "Unsung Hero" award to show you see the impact they make.
- **Leverage free ideas.** And remember, appreciation doesn't have to cost a dime; often, the most meaningful gestures are the simplest ones.

Sometimes You Get What You Deserve

Now, back to my fellow trainee. Thirteen years after that training, before I left the federal government in 2020, I checked to see where he had ended up. I assumed he'd be a high-level administrator in the district. Instead, I found out he had encountered a series of self-inflicted employee relations disasters. His KPIs often suffered because he didn't value or appreciate his people. Without appreciation, he couldn't motivate employees to support his goals. Despite being given one last chance and extra training, he never changed. Eventually, he was demoted to postmaster of a tiny rural post office, with just one employee. The one employee? Him. I guess he finally had all the time in the world to focus on "employee appreciation."

Authentic Appreciation

Now for a happier ending, one that shows what *authentic appreciation* really looks like. Authentic appreciation is different from simply "checking the box" with recognition. It's when a manager takes the time to connect with an employee on a personal level, showing that they see and value them as a human being, not just as a performer of tasks.

I once had an amazing HR Director who had a habit of handing out funny, personalized desk nameplates. When I was going through a stressful time, she gave me one that said: *"I'm kind of a big deal."* On the surface, it was lighthearted and funny. But at that moment, it carried so much more weight. It reminded me that I wasn't invisible, that I mattered, and that someone cared enough to notice I needed encouragement. That small, creative act lifted my spirit and reaffirmed why I chose to work at that organization during that time. Every time I saw that nameplate, it served as a daily reminder: *I'm valued here.*

That's the power of authentic appreciation. It builds commitment, restores confidence, and strengthens the bond between employee and leader, especially in the moments when people need it most.

The truth is that leading others is an honor and a privilege. What I've learned, both from my own experiences and from watching others fail, is that employees are not just numbers plugged into an operation to churn out KPIs. Yes, appreciation can drive better business outcomes, but more importantly, employees are human beings who deserve to be valued for who they are. Never lose sight of that. Theodore Roosevelt said it best: *"Nobody cares how much you know until they know how much you care."* My former classmate is a painful example of what happens when you flip that wisdom upside down.

So, here's your mission, if you choose to accept it (cue the *Mission: Impossible[15]* theme): get out there, be authentic, and make appreciation a habit.

Because the truth is, our employees are a big deal. We're lucky to have them on our teams. Let's make sure they feel like it.

End of Article

PunkRocker HR takeaway from article:

In PunkRocker HR, we don't just say thanks, we show authentic appreciation.

Real appreciation goes deeper than recognition programs or metrics. It's not about checking a box or giving out gift cards. It's about slowing down long enough to really see people: their effort, their challenges, and their humanity.

---

[15] Mission: Impossible Theme – Composed by Lalo Schifrin in 1966, the theme's unusual 5/4 time signature and pulsing rhythm made it instantly recognizable. It first appeared with the Mission: Impossible TV series and has carried through every movie adaptation. Today, it's so ingrained in pop culture that most people hum it whenever they're sneaking around—even if it's just raiding the fridge at midnight.

Have you ever felt that too? That moment when someone finally noticed what you put into your work, not just what came out of it? It changes everything, doesn't it?

That's what authentic appreciation does. It's connection over compliance. It's how we remind people that they matter, not just for their output, but for who they are.

When we make appreciation part of our daily rhythm, we send a powerful message: You matter here. And that message does more than motivate, it builds trust, belonging, and a culture where people don't just show up, they care.

That's where the real results begin.

Call to Action:

When was the last time you showed someone on your team authentic appreciation, not for what they produced, but for who they are as a person?

Chapter 8: The Grinch

The night stretched on, the field quiet except for the sound of wind moving through the trees. A deer darted across the distance, paused, and looked at me, almost curious about what I was still doing there. It made me smile. Fittingly, the next article I opened was about that same season of reindeer: Christmastime.

I'd written it a few years ago while leading an Emerging Leaders program. That time of year always makes me reflect a little deeper, and this story captures one of those reflections. A simple Christmas gift from my team reminded me why leadership should always be about people first. It's about resisting the pull of "command and control" and choosing trust, inspiration, and care instead. Because long after the titles fade and the policies change, people remember how you made them feel.

Funny how Christmas always seems to bring my biggest lessons in leadership. Years before, as a mail carrier, I learned what kindness from strangers could do for the heart. But this time, I'd learn what kindness from your team can do for the soul.

Begin Article:

How a Christmas Gift Saved Me from Becoming the Grinch

Recently, while decorating our Christmas tree, my 10-year-old son Brooks noticed an ornament that made him laugh: Santa dressed as a mailman. He asked me where it came from, and to my surprise, I couldn't remember at first. Like many Christmas ornaments, it had a story behind it. Later that night, when the house was quiet, I looked again at that ornament, and suddenly the memory came flooding back.

So, grab some eggnog, sit by the fireplace, because, as my wife likes to joke, "Looks like it's story time with John!" Let me tell you about the Christmas gift that saved me from becoming the Grinch.

It was Christmas 2007. Six months earlier, I'd been promoted from mail carrier to supervisor at my post office after years of walking the routes. During that time, I'd seen plenty of supervisors come and go. Many fell into the same traps: micromanaging, talking down to people, or clinging to rigid, top-down control. They made sure carriers and clerks knew who was "in charge," but often forgot that their people had lives and families beyond the uniform.

I promised myself that if I ever became a supervisor, I'd do it differently.

So, when I got the chance, I leaned into a leadership style built on trust, respect, and humanity. Yes, my title had changed, but I made sure my team knew we were still in it together, serving customers and going home at the end of the day with peace of mind. I wasn't afraid to set expectations, give feedback, or hold people accountable. But I wanted people to feel valued as human beings, not just as numbers on a schedule.

And for the most part, it worked. Attendance improved, safety incidents declined, morale lifted, and the numbers spoke for themselves.

But my postmaster didn't see it that way. He was a command-and-control type. To him, my approach was too "friendly," and he never hesitated to tell me so. The tension between us made that first Christmas as a supervisor a hard one.

Then came another blow. That December, my wife and I discovered our apartment's storage unit had been broken into. All of our Christmas decorations, including the ones from our first year of marriage, were gone. Many of them were irreplaceable, and my wife was devastated.

The next day at work, an employee asked what was wrong. I mentioned the theft in passing and that we'd need to buy new decorations. I didn't think much more of it.

Until Christmas Eve.

That morning, I walked into my office to find a pile of brand-new ornaments on my desk. Right on top was the Santa-as-a-mailman ornament that now hangs on our tree. Alongside them was a handwritten note:

"Thank you for not changing who you are. We appreciate you. Merry Christmas."

It was from some of my carriers and clerks.

They had quietly come together, knowing what had been stolen and knowing the criticism I'd faced for my leadership style, and decided to remind me I was on the right track.

Have you ever had someone believe in you at just the right moment, when you were starting to doubt yourself? That's what this team did for me.

I was floored. Their kindness pulled me back from the brink of doubting myself.

At our morning safety meeting, I thanked them. The postmaster, true to form, wasn't impressed. He glanced at the ornaments on my desk, rolled his eyes and muttered, "It won't last." The truth is, he didn't last. Two months later, he retired.

Looking back, I realize that without that gift, I might have let his voice drown out mine. I might have abandoned the leadership style that had been working, trading it for something colder and harsher. In other words, I might have become the very thing I promised I wouldn't: a Grinch.

Those ornaments, especially that Santa mailman, remind me every year why staying true to your values matters. They remind me that leadership is about people, not titles. It's about kindness, not control.

Seventeen years later, when Brooks asked about the ornament, I told him the story. After listening closely, he thought for a second and said, "Wow. What a Grinch!"

I said, "Yes, the person who stole our ornaments was a Grinch."

"No," he said. "Your boss was the real Grinch!"

That team gave me one of the greatest Christmas gifts of all, not something you buy in a store, but their belief in me. That gift didn't just restore my faith in people; it restored my faith in myself. They reminded me that kindness in leadership matters. Merry Christmas to you and your family!

End Article

PunkRocker HR takeaway from article:

"In PunkRocker HR, we don't measure leadership by control, we measure it by care."

That Christmas story reminded me that leadership isn't about titles, rules, or proving who's in charge. It's about choosing care over control, even when everything around you pressures you to do the opposite.

Have you ever felt that too? The pressure to change your approach to fit what others expect, even when your gut tells you to lead with compassion instead?

Real leadership doesn't hide behind policies; it leans into humanity. As Theodore Roosevelt said, "Nobody cares how much you know until they know how much you care."

Those carriers proved that with a few ornaments and a handwritten note, reminding me that kindness in leadership doesn't just build teams, it builds trust. That's the difference between leaders people obey and leaders they'll always remember.

Lying in that field, I realized that real, human care isn't weakness; it's strength that grows stronger when it's shared.

Call to Action:

In your leadership today, are you clinging to control, or showing the kind of care that people will remember long after the policies fade?

Chapter 9: Be Curious, Not Judgmental

      I began to pace around the field, reading these articles on my phone. I wondered if anybody could see me walking around this field like an idiot reading my own articles on a dimly lit cell phone. If so, they were probably curious about what I was up to. Speaking of curiosity, that's what the next article I read was all about.

      I wrote this article a few years back while facilitating an Emerging Leaders program. Around that same time, I stumbled onto a TV show and found myself drawn to a character who perfectly captured the spirit of what this human approach to performance management was all about. In the article, I found a lesson that stretched far beyond HR policy or leadership frameworks, something that spoke to the heart of PunkRocker HR and to how we live our lives.

Begin Article:

Be Curious, Not Judgmental

One of my favorite TV shows is *Ted Lasso*. If you aren't familiar, it's about Ted Lasso, an American college football coach from Wichita, Kansas, who gets hired to coach AFC Richmond, an English soccer team. Ted is constantly ridiculed for his folksy, optimistic style and his lack of knowledge about soccer. Over time, though, he wins people over through kindness, empathy, and his unconventional approach to coaching.

In one episode, Ted is challenged to a game of darts by a man who dismisses him as an American idiot. Confident he'll win, the man bets against Ted. By the end of the match, it looks like Ted is behind, and the crowd mocks him for being on the verge of losing. Then Ted shares a story: he actually does know how to play darts because he played with his father every Sunday until his dad passed away. With that, he nails a string of bullseyes and wins.

As he throws the final dart, Ted leaves the crowd with one of the most powerful lines of the series:

"Be curious, not judgmental."

That line has stuck with me. Looking back, it reminds me of some lessons I learned as a father, and an HR professional.

Being Curious, Not Judgmental with Cheesecake

Recently, I learned Ted Lasso's words of wisdom about leaning into curiosity before judgment in my own kitchen. We went to the Cheesecake Factory one night, and I brought home a slice of Reese's Peanut Butter cheesecake. I left it in the fridge and said to myself, *"This will be a great treat for me to enjoy when I get off work tomorrow."* I even explicitly told my kids that if anyone touched my slice of Reese's cheesecake before I got home from work, there would be heck to pay.

All day at work the next day, I thought about that piece of cheesecake. I couldn't wait to get home, kick off my shoes, and demolish it. When I got home, the house was empty; my wife and kids must have gone out somewhere. No worries. I was on a mission: eat my cheesecake.

I opened the fridge, and to my disbelieving eyes, the cheesecake was gone. Vanished. I started to flip out. *One of those kids ate it,* I thought. After I specifically told them not to touch it, they ate it anyway. I was both heartbroken and mad. I texted my wife in a panic: *"Which one of those brats ate my cheesecake?!"* No response. An hour passed. Still nothing.

Finally, I decided on revenge. I was passing judgment on those little stinkers for eating my cheesecake. I opened the pantry and saw their favorite cereals, Cookie Crisp and Golden Grahams. In a binge of revenge, I ate the rest of both boxes. That's right, I poured them together, ate a massive bowl, and emptied both boxes just to prove a point.

Shortly thereafter, my wife and kids came home. They had gone to see a movie, and my wife finally saw my text. "Sorry," she said, "I was cleaning the fridge and put your cheesecake in the freezer so it wouldn't go bad. It's still in there."

I looked in the freezer. And sure enough, there it was. My precious cheesecake. I immediately regretted everything. I had been so quick to judgment. If I had just waited, if I had just been curious instead of assuming, I would've saved myself from looking like an idiot.

Then suddenly, I heard my kids shriek as they opened the pantry. *"Who ate all of our Cookie Crisp and Golden Grahams?!"* My wife turned to me with the most disappointed look on her face. She knew exactly what I had done.

"Kids," she said with a sigh, "Dad's cheesecake is yours."

The mistake I made was that instead of pausing to be curious and consider all the possible alternatives, I was quick to judge based on my own biases. That's how we all get into trouble—at home, at work, anywhere.

That lesson applies far beyond HR. Whether it's with employees, your kids, your spouse, or anyone else you're trying to understand, curiosity paired with consistent, open dialogue builds stronger trust. Judgment, silence, or delayed feedback usually does the opposite.

Being Curious, Not Judgmental at Work

Ted Lasso's words also impacted me at work. A leader came to me during my time in the federal government about a direct report who had always been a rock-star performer, but in the last 30 days had fallen off. This employee, usually sharp and dependable, had missed an important deadline that delayed a customer project, and the client wasn't happy.

The leader told me, "I have to do something about "P." His work has been slipping. I already addressed one missed deadline in a one-on-one, and then the next week he missed another. He just seems different. I think it's time to put him on a performance improvement plan, so he knows he needs to shape up or ship out."

I could tell the leader was frustrated and ready to jump straight into judgment. But I felt there was an important step missing. This leader was great at driving high performance but struggled at times with emotional intelligence and reading the room. He knew this was an area of growth for him, but under pressure he defaulted to operational focus and forgot about the humanity of his people.

Later that day, while making my rounds, something I often did to keep HR approachable, I stopped by P's office. Normally we'd trade dad jokes, but that day he didn't laugh like he usually did. I shook his hand and walked away, but one detail stuck out to me.

When I met again with the leader, I asked, "P's been a rockstar for you for over five years. These issues only started this past month?"

"Yes," he said.

"In your one-on-ones lately, I bet you've focused heavily on his missed deadlines and laying out your expectations?"

"Exactly," he replied.

I nodded, then asked a curious question. "Doesn't it seem odd that a top performer suddenly changes like this? Have you asked him, 'How are you doing? How's your wife and kids? Everything okay at home?'"

The leader admitted he hadn't. "We've been so busy, I've just been focused on the work."

I told him, "When I shook his hand earlier, I noticed he wasn't wearing his wedding ring. I don't know what's going on, and it's none of my business, but the curious human in me wonders if things at home might be affecting him at work."

The leader paused, then looked at me and asked, "So what do I do?"

"Since P has always been open about his family, I don't think it would cross a boundary to ask. Go into his office, ask if he has a moment, and simply say, 'Are you okay? How are things on the home front?' If he opens up, remind him about EAP and free counseling, and that he can take as much leave as needed to work through whatever's going on. If it's something that could qualify for FMLA, let me know and I'll sit with him too. Just be curious and give him a chance to share if he chooses."

The leader followed through and had the conversation. It turned out P and his wife had temporarily separated, and he was really struggling. The leader realized the pressure of work combined with his personal life was throwing him completely off balance. Instead of handing him a performance improvement plan, the leader offered support: EAP, time off, and space to heal.

P accepted the help, took a few weeks off, got counseling, and eventually returned to work. While I don't know if his marriage was restored, the leader told me that P came back reenergized and quickly returned to his rock-star performance.

Later, the leader admitted that if he had pushed forward with the performance plan instead of choosing curiosity, P likely would have quit on the spot. That was how close he was to the edge. But because the leader paused and leaned into curiosity first, he got a better outcome for P, for the team, and for the business.

And for the leader, it was a lesson he carried forward: judgment first can break people; curiosity first can save them.

Curious about Talent

One final example of curiosity over judgment from my time in the federal government involved a gentleman I'll call "D." D was in his early to mid-50s, well known around the organization. Everyone agreed he was a solid worker on his team, dependable, skilled, and hardworking. But he also had a reputation as a bit of a joker. Because of that, some people didn't take him seriously.

One day, after his supervisor announced he would be retiring in a few years, D came to me and said he was interested in stepping into that supervisor role. When I shared this with a few leaders, their reaction was predictable: they rolled their eyes. "D isn't serious," they said. "He doesn't have what it takes."

But instead of being judgmental, I got curious.

Whenever someone comes to me for coaching about their career growth, I test their seriousness. I like to give them a challenge: something concrete that requires effort and follow-through. So, I sat down with D and pulled out the supervisor's current job description. Together, we walked through it and identified the key skills he would need to strengthen over the next year to show he could do that job and be a worthy candidate if he applied. From that, I helped him put together a draft Professional Growth and Development Plan (PGDP).

One major gap stood out: computer skills, especially Microsoft Excel. So, I laid down a challenge. "Here's the deal," I told him. "I've got an open beginner-to-intermediate Excel training scheduled on Friday. I encourage you to do two things: (1) finalize this PGDP with your supervisor's signature and return it to me, and (2) sign up for and complete that Excel class. If you do both, I'll know you're serious about becoming a leader."

Not only did D complete his PGDP, but he showed up for that Excel class, the oldest guy in the room, and the only one from a field crew. A few weeks later, he came back to meet with me, eager to share what he had learned and update me on the other areas he was working on. Over time, we kept meeting for coaching, and I watched him start to shift. His approach became more intentional, more professional. And people around him started to notice the change.

In the end, while others judged D and dismissed him as a joker, curiosity allowed me to see something more: grit, growth, and a real hunger to lead that was buried beneath the surface. He wasn't just serious; he was proving it. And I had no doubt that, in time, D would make an excellent supervisor if he kept it up.

Curiosity is the Key

At the end of the day, leaders at every level have a choice: approach people with judgment or approach them with curiosity. Judgment shuts doors; curiosity opens them. And when you pair curiosity with consistent, meaningful conversations, you don't just improve performance reviews; you build trust, engagement, and workplaces where people want to stay and grow.

As you see from the stories above, the lesson works both inside and outside the office. Whether it's trying to figure out why your cheesecake is missing, or why a rock-star employee is suddenly struggling, curiosity will take you further than judgment every time.

So, whether it's at work, at home, or in a pub with a dartboard, remember Ted's words: be curious, not judgmental.

PunkRocker HR takeaway from article:

In PunkRocker HR, we choose curiosity over judgment, every time.

So much of traditional HR pushes us toward judgment. We slot people into performance boxes, label behavior as good or bad, and move on. And sure, sometimes that structure has its place. But curiosity? Curiosity does something different. It builds trust. It opens doors. It helps us understand the "why" behind what people do.

Have you ever felt that too, that urge to jump straight to judgment, when deep down you knew curiosity might lead you somewhere better?

That's what this story reminded me of. "D" eventually got that supervisor job, proof that curiosity can create opportunity in ways judgment never will.

Looking back now, I realize this lesson wasn't just for employees or supervisors, it was for me too. Toward the end of my time as an HR leader, there were moments I felt misunderstood by some leaders. In hindsight, I wish I'd been more curious about their perspective, the pressures they faced, the reasons behind their reactions. Maybe it wouldn't have changed the outcome, but it might have changed how I carried it.

Call to Action:

When you're faced with a tough decision that could go either way, ask yourself: Am I being curious, or am I being judgmental?

Chapter 10: Lessons in Leadership and Vulnerability

At this point, I lay back down in the same spot in the field, staring up at the night sky. The next article I read was one I wrote a few years back after a conversation with one of my emerging leaders who asked me a simple but heavy question: "What does it really take to be a great leader?" Leadership, in my opinion, is one of the most oversaturated topics out there. Everyone seems to have the "right" formula, the perfect checklist, or the quick-fix blueprint. And maybe no one truly does. I'm honest enough to admit that while I've had some wins as a leader, I've also had some failures. There are days I've walked out of meetings thinking, "What the heck am I doing?" And there are nights I've lain awake, replaying my conversations in my head wondering, "Did I say the right thing there?"

But here's the thing: we keep showing up anyway. Because leadership isn't about being flawless; it's about learning as you go, adjusting when you get it wrong, and having the humility to grow in real time, even when people are watching. That's messy, but it's also real. My hope in writing this piece is that others can see both the cracks and the lessons in my journey, and maybe, just maybe, find something in my mistakes that helps them in theirs.

From the Mound to the Workplace: Lessons in Leadership and Vulnerability

I was recently asked by an emerging leader at my organization, "What is the most important skill an emerging leader should develop right now?"

I was taken aback because there are so many important skills a leader should develop. There are many TED Talks, TikToks, and Harvard Business Review articles detailing the skills needed to be a great leader today. As I thought about it, I could name many skills, such as empathy, active listening, inclusivity, and many more, but not one skill alone stood out.

When I got home from work that day, my wife was scrapbooking some old photos, and I noticed she had some old pictures of me from high school. One was me in my high school baseball uniform. As I stared at that picture, a forgotten lesson from the pitcher's mound came rushing back.

Vulnerability on the Mound

It was April 1996. I was 16 years old, pitching for my high school baseball team, the Howard Lions. I loved pitching, standing on the mound, ball in hand, staring into the eyes of the batter and giving it everything I had to throw that ball by them.

We were playing Hammond High School, and I was having one of my best pitching performances. I remember this particular day it was a humid, hazy afternoon with storm clouds brewing on the horizon. My fastball command was spot on, and I was dropping in my knuckle-curve well. We were up 2–1 until the fifth inning when I ran into some trouble. I walked two batters in a row to load the bases, and I felt like the umpire wasn't giving me the strike zone on the outside corner. I was punching my glove and giving the ump dirty looks after each walk—my frustration visible for all to see.

Then, suddenly, the rain started to come down. Not hard enough for the umpire to pause the game, but hard enough that I could feel my grip on the ball begin to slip a bit. Then I looked behind the backstop, and there stood my dad. I had no idea he had shown up to the game during that inning. He was very busy running an auto repair shop and rarely came to my games, but there he was, on this day, standing in his auto shop uniform with his arms folded, with rain falling on all of us. He moved behind the backstop to get my attention. He then motioned with his two fingers to his eyes, then to me, as if to say, "Hey, I'm watching you, so cut it out."

I was already frustrated, so I didn't need my dad back there adding fuel to the fire. So, standing on the mound, with the rain dripping off the bill of my cap, I stared at my dad. With my next pitch, I heaved it as hard as I could, four feet to the right, and the ball hit the metal backstop right in front of his face with a loud "bang." The umpire and batter just assumed it was a wild pitch, and my teammates thought it was hilarious. That made me smile and feel better, so I proceeded to strike the batter out to end the inning and I headed to the dugout. As I got to the dugout, my father motioned for me to come to the opening, where he grabbed me by the shirt and pulled me toward his face. He then looked me in the eyes and said, "Never let them see you sweat. You hear me? Never let them see you sweat."

After he told me that, I proceeded to finish the game, and we got the win. However, my father's words of "never let them see you sweat" stayed with me into my adulthood. To me, his words "never let them see you sweat" were about being tough and never letting your emotions or imperfections show in all circumstances; otherwise, you will appear to be weak.

These words followed me into my professional life, which I think helped me stay even-handed and calm in many chaotic situations. But for a long time, and into my tenure as an operations supervisor, this caused me to build up a bit of an emotional wall. I never showed much emotion (besides laughing at a good joke).

Vulnerability Leads to Trust

Fast forward many years later, into my 30s, I was working in HR. I was working with an HR Director at my federal agency whom I didn't know very well just yet, and I was still trying to figure him out. One day, I was scheduled to have a meeting with him. When we met, I could see he wasn't himself. He was honest and said, "You know what, John? I don't think I can do this today. Honestly, I've had a few tough days at home, and I'm not the best version of myself today. If you don't mind, could we reschedule this?"

I was taken aback that he would share that with me. I was moved to see that this leader was a human just like me, who had home struggles like me, who at times wasn't the best version of himself like me. He allowed himself to let me "see him sweat." In other words, he allowed himself to be vulnerable with me. After that day, and I couldn't explain it at the time, I felt my trust for him grow and would have run through a wall for him as my leader.

80

Speaking Vulnerability

While I wouldn't say it's the most important, I think being vulnerable is one of the more important skills a great leader can develop in today's climate. Over the last few years, I have learned that as a leader, you don't have to be perfect or have all the answers. In fact, it's okay to say things like:

"I'm not sure I know the answer to that. Let's figure it out together."

"I've never seen this before."

"I'm struggling a bit today."

"This week was tough for me."

"You know what? I made a mistake here. I have to be better."

What I've learned is that displaying vulnerability from time to time lets our team know that we are human beings just like them. We know we're not perfect, we don't have all the answers, we have hard days, and we need grace from time to time just like them. It's okay for them to see that on occasion.

The questions you may have are: what is too vulnerable, and how often should we be vulnerable? In my experience, it's one of those things that you know when you see it. Boundaries are still important, and TMI (Too Much Information) can quickly go from being vulnerable to creating awkward moments. Trust your intuition as a leader and your knowledge of your team members.

For some, this skill may come easier to develop than for others. And if I may tiptoe into the controversial, depending on when you were raised, and especially for males, displaying vulnerability can be difficult. My dad was a Navy veteran of the Vietnam War era and always believed in displaying "toughness." He raised me to believe showing emotion or vulnerability as a man was a sign of weakness. But as I have grown into a leader, I believe when used correctly, vulnerability is a great strength of a leader.

I've also learned the importance of vulnerability as a leader, especially when leading teams that include Millennials and Gen Z employees. You don't need to be the loudest voice in meetings or appear to be the smartest person in the room to influence them. From my experience, they care less about how tough or perfect you are; instead, what matters to them is how human and relatable you are. They are more open to constructive feedback from someone who shows their own imperfections from time to time.

Call to Action

In closing, the other day I was watching a baseball game with my nine-year-old son. In the game, a pitcher was cruising until the 7th inning when he gave up a three-run home run that gave the other team the lead. The pitcher was taken out of the game. When he got to the bench, the camera showed him slamming his glove down and sitting on the bench with a towel over his head, upset, as teammates slapped him on the back to console him. My son, seeing this, said, "Well, that's embarrassing! Doesn't he know he's on camera looking upset like that?"

I flashed back to that day many years ago on the pitching mound in high school in the rain, heaving baseballs at my dad's head in frustration. I thought about what my dad said, then what I learned about vulnerability from my former HR director. I told my son, "It's okay. He's not hurting anyone, just showing a bit of emotion due to his passion. That's okay, right?"

"Oh, I get it, Dad," he said. "Like the other night when the closer blew the game in the ninth inning and you cursed at the TV and said the manager should be fired?"

Touché. I wasn't the best version of myself that day either.

There are many skills that can make us great leaders. Developing the skill of being vulnerable when appropriate is one of them. Considering our own human nature, embracing and displaying vulnerability as needed might just be the key to truly connecting with and inspiring the human beings we lead.

End Article

PunkRocker HR takeaway from article:

In PunkRocker HR, we know that true strength comes from vulnerability.

Maybe you have heard that good leaders don't show cracks; that we're supposed to be composed, confident, and always in control. But the truth is, people don't connect with perfect. They connect with real.

Here's something real: one of the hardest parts of embracing PunkRocker HR is being vulnerable enough to admit when we've fallen short. Even with the best intentions, something we say or do can land in a way we never meant, and it can quietly turn down the volume on humanity. Have you ever felt that? It hurts as a leader, especially when you lead with heart, to learn that your actions may have unintentionally hurt someone else's.

Long after I left a role a while back, I learned that a member of my team had been hurt by a something I said and a decision I made. My intentions were good, but it didn't land that way, and that realization broke my heart. If I ever see them again, I'll make sure to own it. Humility is accepting that, from time to time, we will fall short. Vulnerability is being willing to acknowledge it, and choosing to do better next time.

It is time to reject the old-school idea that leaders have to be flawless or stoic. Real leadership lets people see you sweat sometimes because it shows them you're human too. Vulnerability builds trust, connection, and loyalty in ways no policy or KPI ever could.

That's PunkRocker HR.

Call to Action:

When was the last time you let your team see your humanity instead of your perfection?

Chapter 11: Planes, Trains, and Automobiles

As I lay in the field, I took a break from the articles and opened Facebook. I began to go through old photos of me and the family. One was a recent Thanksgiving photo with my wife and kids. This photo warmed my heart. It reminded me of an article I wrote about Thanksgiving.

The next article I read I wrote a few years back as I reflected on Thanksgiving and the meaning of family. For most of us, work isn't our dream job; it's the way we provide for the people we love. But too often, the sacrifices we make on the job leave us so drained that by the time we walk through the front door, there's not much left for the ones who matter most. The obstacles aren't just late trains, tough deadlines, or unexpected disruptions; they are the stress and exhaustion that slowly steal our peace. But what if it didn't have to be that way? What if we could carry our sense of peace through the grind, because we remembered that our families deserve the best of us first?

Begin Article:

Planes, Trains, and the Journey Home: What Really Matters in Life

The last time I watched Planes, Trains, and Automobiles[16], I was in my early twenties. It was two decades ago, before marriage, kids, and the balancing act of adulthood. Back then, I thought it was funny, full of brilliant comedic moments from John Candy and Steve Martin.

---

[16] Planes, Trains and Automobiles (1987) is a comedy film starring Steve Martin and John Candy. It follows two mismatched travelers struggling through a series of misadventures as they try to make it home for Thanksgiving, highlighting themes of patience, empathy, and unlikely friendship.

Scenes like "Those aren't pillows!" stuck with me. But I didn't understand why so many people revered it. Sure, it was nice that Neil Page (played by Steve Martin) made it home in time for Thanksgiving, but what made this movie iconic?

Fast forward 20 years: I'm now in my early forties, married with kids, navigating the complexities of career, family, and that elusive thing we call "balance." Life is a series of priorities in tension, trying to succeed at work, provide for my family, and still be present for the moments that matter. My body feels a little achier, my patience thinner, and the weight of midlife a little heavier.

The other day, while waiting for my vehicle to be serviced, I found myself with a couple of hours to kill. All I wanted was to get home in time for dinner with my wife and kids. Sitting in the customer waiting room, I was restless, my mind spinning with the usual midlife pressures. Work emails I should be answering, the never-ending home improvement projects I hadn't tackled, and a new ache in my back that seemed to whisper, "You're not as young as you used to be." Then, I glanced up at the TV and saw Planes, Trains, and Automobiles playing. I hadn't seen it in 20 years. Figuring it would be a decent distraction, I settled in. What I didn't expect was for it to land so differently this time, hitting me in ways I hadn't felt before.

From the opening scene, I was hooked. Suddenly, I was Neil Page (interesting, I am now the same age Steve Martin was as he played this character). I felt his frustration, sitting in a mind-numbing work meeting in New York City, anxiously watching the clock, desperate to catch his flight and get home to his family in Chicago. I understood the deep yearning to get somewhere meaningful, only to be thwarted by stolen cabs, flight delays, and a well-meaning but maddening travel companion, Del Griffith.

Take the scene where Neil loses it on the rental car agent. The car he reserved isn't there, and after nearly getting himself killed trying to return to the rental counter, he snaps. His frustration, raw, unfiltered, and painfully relatable, spills out. As I watched, I caught myself whispering, "Get her, Neil!" We've all been there, haven't we? Fighting against obstacles we didn't create, just wanting to get home.

Then there's the moment Neil explodes at Del, mocking him for being an obnoxious storyteller and a less-than-hygienic travel companion (those socks in the sink!). Del's response, though, cuts through the noise:

"I like me."

It's a quiet reminder that we aren't alone in our struggle to get home; everyone's fighting their own battles, trying to make sense of their imperfections along the way. It's not just about getting home; it's about the people we meet on the journey home and what they teach us about grace.

Then, of course, there's the ending, the moment that ties it all together. Neil finally makes it home, walking through the door just in time for Thanksgiving dinner. After days of chaos, missed connections, and mounting frustration, he sees his kids rushing toward him, their excitement palpable. Then he locks eyes with his wife across the room, her eyes glistening with tears of relief and joy. They hadn't spoken in days (this was the '80s, no texts, no quick calls to check in). In that moment, everything else, work meetings, travel mishaps, every obstacle along the way, fades into the background. The only thing that matters is being with the people he loves most. As they embrace, you realize the journey wasn't just about getting home; it was about rediscovering what home truly means.

Looking back, when I first got married in my twenties, I took Thanksgiving for granted. I was of the mind that there would always be another chance to gather with family, whether it was my parents or my wife's parents. But five years ago, my wife lost her parents. They were only in their late fifties. Now, every Thanksgiving, I see the pain in my wife's eyes. She wishes she could go home to them, but that home no longer exists. Watching Planes, Trains, and Automobiles reminded me how fleeting these moments to go home are. And why it is so important to do all we can to get home to embrace these moments, no matter the obstacles.

In my teens, I couldn't wait to leave home. Now, in my forties, all I want is to get back there—not to a physical house, but to the people who make it home. My wife. My kids. My parents. My sisters. That movie hit me like a truth I already knew but had forgotten: We spend so much of our lives chasing success that we lose sight of what success actually means.

The movie also reframed how I see obstacles. The "Del Griffiths" in our lives: the delays, distractions, and disruptions are frustrating. However, they're also teachers. They remind us to slow down, laugh at the absurdity of it all, and realign with what truly matters. Neil's journey wasn't just about getting home; it was about learning to appreciate the messiness of life and the humanity in others who share our journey.

Another thing I learned, and that this movie reminded me of, is to slow down and enjoy the moment. Like many people, I get excited for the holidays in December, the lights, the music, the celebrations. But in that rush, we sometimes treat Thanksgiving like a hurdle we just have to clear before the "real" holidays begin. That's what makes Thanksgiving so special. It forces us to pause, take a breath, and recognize what we're truly thankful for: the obstacles and the triumphs, the laughter and the lessons, and most of all, the people who make the journey worth it.

To my fellow Millennials, we're not kids anymore. Growing up, we were often reminded to be "thankful" this time of year. But this year, I encourage you to be grateful for more than just the people around the table. Be thankful for the daily journey it takes to get home to them. Because in a way, we're all on that journey every single day, aren't we? We're all just trying to get home to the ones we love.

This Thanksgiving, a 40-year-old movie reminded me of life's simplest truth: cherish not just the people you love but also the path that brings you together. The obstacles, whether it's a broken-down train or a traveling companion who thinks your thighs are two warm pillows, aren't just hurdles: they're part of the story. In the end, life isn't measured by our career accomplishments, possessions, or social status. It's measured in love given, memories made, and the stories shared over a slice of pumpkin pie with the ones who make the journey worthwhile.

So, this Thanksgiving, hold tight to what truly matters: the people sitting at your table.

And embrace the journey that brings you home to them.

End of Article

PunkRocker HR takeaway from article:

In PunkRocker HR, the real measure of success is employees going home with peace and purpose.

Have you ever ended a workday feeling completely spent — like you had nothing left to give the people who matter most? I've been there too. In HR, helping people "get home" isn't just about clocking out; it's about making sure they have the energy and peace to actually live once they do.

Peace comes from knowing their workplace is fair, supportive, and safe. Purpose comes from knowing their work means something. PunkRocker HR doesn't just talk about "work-life balance." We fight for it. Because the truest measure of leadership isn't in output or performance metrics — it's in whether people can leave work whole, not hollow.

That's the rebellion. Transactional HR says, "Can we do more with less?"

PunkRocker HR says, "Go home with enough."

Just like in Planes, Trains, and Automobiles, the journey may be messy, but it's in the mess that we find what matters most, and it's what makes the arrival home that much sweeter.

Call to Action:

Are your employees or teammates going home drained and empty, or with the peace and purpose they need to give their best selves to the people who matter most?

Chapter 12: Bridge the Gap

As I continued to lie in the field, I thought about an incident a few months before resigning from my job. My new boss had expressed a desire to see different generations at the company begin to mesh. In response, I wrote an article about how those generations could come together, listen, and do great work.

That was the next article I read. I was just beginning to realize how much relationships drive everything in an organization, and how much intention it takes to create real harmony across them. One of the biggest challenges ahead for today's workforce is helping generations find that harmony. It isn't easy, but it's possible.

As HR leaders, our job isn't just to bridge the gap between executives and employees. It's also to recognize the generational dynamics within those groups and find ways for them to complement rather than clash. To me, it's a lot like mixing two songs at once. Mission impossible? Maybe. But with a little grace, and a little space, the mix can work.

Begin Article:

HR's New Role: Bridge the Gap

It was the summer of 1997, that sweaty, restless stretch before my senior year of high school. My older cousin Bobby, a thirty-something concrete construction boss out of Baltimore, decided I needed a taste of real life and a paycheck, so he threw me on his crew. The goal? Save enough for a beat-up car I had my eye on.

I showed up that first June morning on Wilkins Avenue with no clue what I was walking into. If you've ever lived through a Baltimore summer, you know the air is thick, the humidity is unforgiving, and the heat sticks to you like a second skin. The work hit me like a sledgehammer, literally. Most mornings started with busting up old sidewalks or patios, swinging a jackhammer until my arms felt like rubber. Then came hauling endless chunks of busted-up concrete into a dump truck. If we didn't have a mix truck that day, we mixed concrete by hand and wheeled it over in wheelbarrows, cursing the Baltimore summer sun with every load.

But what I remember most wasn't the heat, it was the crew. We were four guys spanning decades. At 16, I was the kid. Bo, in his early 20s, was full of restless energy. Bobby, my cousin in his 30s, ran the show with grit and a grin. And Scottie, pushing 40, was the grizzled veteran who'd seen it all. Each day someone got to play DJ. Scottie blasted Zeppelin and Skynyrd. Bobby leaned into punk and hair metal. Bo brought early '90s rap like Dr. Dre and Snoop Dogg. And me? I tuned in alternative, Blink-182, Third Eye Blind, the soundtrack of my teenage angst.

We tore into each other constantly. "This isn't music, it's garbage!" But by summer's end, something had shifted. Scottie was tapping his foot to Blink-182, and I caught myself humming along to "Stairway to Heaven." The gap didn't disappear, but it shrank. Turns out, sweating side by side and sharing a boombox will do that.

Fast forward to now: decades later, I'm leading an HR team, and I'm right back on another crew, this time bridging gaps between generations in the workplace. They call me an "Xennial," stuck between analog-loving Gen X and the tech-savvy Millennials. I grew up with a Walkman in one hand and a dial-up modem at home. Today, I stand in the middle of a corporate bridge, with Millennials and Gen Z on one side, Boomers and Gen X on the other. And like back in '97, we're all trying to work together, chasing the same goals but sometimes stepping on each other's toes.

The challenge? We need to bridge the gap. Not just hear each other but listen. Younger generations at times may want to rewrite the rules. However, older generations built the foundation we're standing on. My job as an HR leader is to make sure the new voices don't drown out wisdom, and the veterans don't write off the new crowd as spoiled or clueless. Oh, and deliver business results while I'm at it. No pressure, right?

Here's the good news: it's not impossible. We can make this work. After years of trial and error, I've learned it comes down to two simple things: grace and space. Give the new generations room to grow and give the old guard credit for what they've built.

The Generational Remix: Equalize the Playlist

Picture your workplace as a playlist. The Baby Boomers are the classic rock anthems, gritty and soulful, the backbone of the setlist. Gen X is the alt-rock rebels, sharp and resourceful, turning chaos into something lasting. Millennials bring the pop energy: bold, collaborative, and obsessed with meaning. And Gen Z? They're the streaming-era disruptors, pushing boundaries and unafraid to remix everything.

Right now, all these tracks are playing at once, and they're not always in harmony. Pew Research tells us this is the first time in modern history we've had five generations in the workforce: Silent Generation holdouts, Boomers, Gen X, Millennials, and Gen Z. Each brings its own quirks. Millennials and Gen Z crave flexibility and purpose and adapt quickly. They're the ones asking, "Why are we still doing it this way?" Gen X and Boomers value loyalty and results. They're more likely to say, "We've done it this way for decades, and it works."

The clash isn't just anecdotal. Deloitte found Millennials and Gen Z are twice as likely as older generations to prioritize work-life balance and social impact over pay or promotions. Meanwhile, SHRM research shows Boomers and Gen X often feel overlooked as younger workers rise. Everyone's blasting their track, but nobody's mixing the playlist.

The C-Suite Shift: Credit the Veterans

Leadership is shifting fast. For decades, Boomers and Gen X shaped the table, climbing ladders, putting in late nights, and building the companies we're now reimagining. But Millennials are stepping into VP and C-suite roles. By 2025, they'll make up 75% of the workforce, with Gen Z right behind them, bringing digital fluency and impatience with red tape.

This shift is both a breath of fresh air and a potential storm. Younger leaders push for remote work, flatter structures, and tech adoption. A McKinsey report found 70% of Millennials and Gen Z want organizations to embrace new tools and approaches, compared to just 40% of Boomers. Innovation often comes from discomfort, but it must be balanced. Work isn't adult daycare. Deadlines still need hitting. Clients still need serving. Change without results is noise.

The HR Leader's Tightrope

If you're in HR, you know this feeling: walking a tightrope. On one side, you've got Millennials and Gen Z clamoring for their shot, sometimes calling out practices as unfair or outdated. On the other, you've got Boomers and Gen X who've poured decades into building stability and don't want to be dismissed. Above you, executives just want the numbers to add up.

It's tempting to paper over the cracks, but ignoring tension doesn't make it go away. *Harvard Business Review* found that generational conflict lingers if it isn't addressed head-on. So how do we bridge it? For me, it always comes back to grace and space.

Grace: The Art of Cutting Some Slack

Let's start with the younger crowd. Millennials and Gen Z can (at times) be a lot, vocal, idealistic, sometimes rough around the edges. They'll question policies in a meeting or send you a TED Talk about "reinventing work." And sure, it's easy to roll your eyes. But here's the thing: they're not wrong to speak up. MIT research shows diverse teams, age included, outperform others in innovation by 35%.

They just need grace. Professionalism isn't instinctive, it's learned. I once mentored a Gen Z employee who fired off an email to the President of the organization that came across more like a demand than a suggestion. I pulled them aside: "Your idea's great, but let's talk about how to pitch it." Their passion was real; they just needed coaching. Grace is meeting people where they are, not where you think they should already be.

Flip it: Boomers and Gen X deserve grace too. They built the systems we're all tweaking. When they resist change, it's not always stubbornness, it's battle scars. One Boomer told me, "I've seen a lot of 'game changers' flop." He wasn't being negative; he was drawing on experience. Listening to that doesn't stall progress. It builds a stronger base to push off from.

Space: Room to Grow, Room to Contribute

Grace sets the tone. Space makes it real. For younger workers, space means ownership. Don't just hear their ideas, give them a pilot project. Whether it flies or flops, they'll learn more from the experience than from a lecture.

For Boomers and Gen X, space means unleashing expertise. Pair them with younger colleagues, not as "mentors on the sidelines," but as co-creators. I've seen this done: Boomers guiding Gen Z through process discipline, Gen Z teaching them data tricks. Costs dropped 15%. Both sides felt valued. That's space. This leads to what I call *reverse mentoring*, where the older mentor can grow as much as the younger mentee as they learn from each other in this relationship.

This is where HR has to step up. Execs can bristle when younger voices push against the status quo. But instead of shutting it down, ask: "Why do you feel that way?" That question, rooted in curiosity rather than defense, can turn friction into insight. With Millennials and Gen Z making up three-quarters of the workforce by decade's end, executives who ignore them risk steering a ship with the sails tied. HR's job is to help them hear the wind and adjust the sails together.

The Call to Action: HR, It's Your Moment

This generational mash-up isn't a problem, it's a chance. HR leaders, you're the DJs. Your job isn't to play favorites or mute anyone's track. It's to mix the playlist so everyone hears something they love while the beat keeps driving forward.

One caution: not every generational stereotype sticks. I've met Boomers who crave flexibility and Gen Zers who grind like it's 1985. Labels are easy. People are complex. Research from the Journal of

Organizational Behavior shows individual differences often outweigh generational ones. So, use those broad brushes lightly. Real magic happens when you see people as individuals first, generations second.

So, here's the challenge: tomorrow, pick one team. Listen, really listen, to what each generation is saying. Give the newbies grace to stumble. Give the vets space to shine. Bring what you learn back to the top. It won't be clean. It'll be messy, human, and worth it.

Bridge the Gap

Back to the summer of 1997. At the end of each blistering day, the four of us, me, Bo, Bobby, and Scottie, would pack up tools and glance back at what we had built. A new sidewalk. A solid patio. A driveway ready for years of use. We were a Mötley Crüe, fighting over music, bickering about technique, but the work got done. That quiet sense of accomplishment of looking back at what we built together always stuck with me.

It's the same thing we're chasing now. In the 2020's and beyond, bridging this generational divide won't always be pretty. The noise, the differences, the push and pull are real. But once we learn to row together, blending the boldness of the young with the wisdom of the seasoned, there's no limit to the work we can accomplish every day, or what we can build together.

So, HR leaders, let's get to it. Listen with grace. Create space. Watch what happens when every generation pulls in the same direction. The gap isn't a wall. It's a bridge. Let's cross it together.

End of Article

PunkRocker HR takeaway from article:

In PunkRocker HR, bridging the gap means putting ourselves in the other person's shoes, every time, even when it hurts.

Have you ever worked with someone whose style or values just didn't line up with yours? The kind of person who makes you bite your tongue in meetings or rethink your patience? I've been there too. It's not easy. But real connection isn't about tolerating differences — it's about empathy. Extending grace. Making the effort to understand what others value, even when it stings a little.

One of the biggest lessons my team taught me by the end of a recent HR role, a team made up of different generations, personalities, and lived experiences, was this: not everyone wants to be led the same way. And if you try to lead everyone the way you want to be led, you'll miss people without even realizing it. You have to slow down, pay attention, and figure how they want to be led. How they prefer to receive feedback. How they prefer recognition. What drains them and what fuels them. That's turning up the humanity on your leadership.

Sometimes the "fun" after-work thing you plan to celebrate a team win isn't all that fun for someone who just wants to get home to their kids. Other times, the quietest person on your team has the best idea, if you make space for them to share it. These small things matter. If we ignore them, we risk turning down the humanity at work without even noticing.

Because when you meet people where they are, the whole environment shifts. Task conflict handled with empathy becomes collaboration. Personality differences become strengths. The goal isn't perfect harmony, it's understanding. That's how teams grow, even through the rough notes.

Call to Action:

When was the last time you truly stepped into a coworker's shoes — not just to understand their role, but to understand what they value and how they want to be led, even when it was uncomfortable?

Chapter 13: Sandlot Salvation

As I lay in the field, I kept reading and realized it was the same one where my son Brooks and I had played catch so many times. That led me to the next article I wrote, right around the start of a baseball season a few years back.

For me, baseball has always been more than a game. It's been a teacher. It's where I first learned about resilience, friendship, and what it feels like to truly belong. Now, as my son grows older, my hope is that if he's interested, he'll get to discover some of those same lessons.

Baseball also shaped the way I lead in HR. It taught me patience, humility, teamwork, and how to bounce back from mistakes, many of the same qualities that define PunkRocker HR. On the flip side, some of the hardest and most painful moments of my life are tied to baseball too. Looking back, I can see how both the trauma and the triumph uncovered one of the most powerful PunkRocker HR traits I carry with me today: the belief that belonging saves people.

Begin Article:

The Sandlot Salvation

Every spring, baseball strolls back into our lives like an old friend we haven't seen in a long time, and we can't wait to hug.

For lots of folks, it's just another American pastime, something to, well, pass the time. For others, it's a burning passion and a boyhood dream that, for a lucky few, turns into a real-life fairy tale and a career in the majors. Some think it's the dullest thing on TV, only worth watching if you're half-drunk. But for me, baseball was a lifeline. It grabbed me when I was sinking and taught me lessons I'll carry forever about friendship, romance, perseverance, and, in the end, the deep pride of being a dad.

Belonging on the Sandlot

My first memory of baseball begins at age six, during a time when my world was starting to come apart. My family (my dad, mom, sister, and older half-brother) lived together in a Baltimore City townhome. My dad was a hardworking auto mechanic, but my parents' relationship had grown strained and unpredictable. I remember nights filled with loud, heated arguments that shook the walls and left my sister and me hiding in our room, unsure of what might happen next. Those moments were frightening for us. Not long after, my parents divorced.

A few years later, my mother disappeared from my life. Her leaving had a profound impact on me as an eight-year-old boy. My dad stepped up and moved us out to Elkridge, Maryland, to escape the wreckage. He remarried, and soon I had more sisters. I had a new mom, a stepmom who did her best, but it was still tough for us. Also, carrying some tough memories, I sank into a quiet, heavy depression as a ten-year-old kid.

Then, one summer day, everything shifted. I was about 11 years old, the new kid in the neighborhood. A group of boys pounded on my front door, shouting: *"Hey man, come play baseball with us!"*

I had barely touched a ball before, but my new friend Clint shoved his extra glove into my hand, another guy John tossed me his spare bat, and off we ran to the sandlot. Day after day, we played, sweaty, laughing, no cares in the world. One afternoon, a kid smashed a ball to the fence. I was in the outfield and with my heart racing, ran over, scooped it up and then fired a laser back to the backstop that nailed the runner at home plate. I had no idea I could throw a baseball that far.

The boys froze. They shouted, *"Did that dude just do that? Holy crap!"*

And just like that, I felt like I finally belonged.

Those boys became my brothers. They were my crew all the way through high school, even when we wore the same junior varsity baseball uniforms. Every spring, when baseball wakes up from its winter slumber, I remember that sandlot and those wild, scrappy kids who dragged me out of the dark. Baseball, and those friends, saved me.

Give that Fan...Your Number?

Fast forward to sophomore year of high school. I was 14. My dad and I went to an Orioles day game at Camden Yards. We landed seats behind home plate, close enough to hear the crack of the bat.

At that age, girls and baseball consumed my every thought. A group of girls sat behind us, one of them was gorgeous, with the kind of smile that makes a guy's heart skip a beat. The guys sitting next to her had way more "game" than me and flirted with her all day. I sat there quietly, clutching my glove like a security blanket.

In the fifth inning, a foul ball screamed back, fast and deadly. My heart jumped, and somehow, I snagged it, inches from the pretty girl's face. She gasped, her friends shrieked. The PA announcer shouted: *"Give that fan a contract!"* Ushers rushed down, scribbling my name to mail me an "off-field fielder" certificate from the Orioles (which eventually did arrive).

But that wasn't the real prize. As we stood to leave, the girl walked right past the guys next to her, stopped in front of me, put her hand on my shoulder, and slipped her phone number into my hand. I learned she lived in Columbia, MD, close enough to see each other. I smirked as those other guys' jaws hit the floor. I would actually get to date that girl for a little while, all thanks to a lucky grab of the baseball…and her phone number.

End it on Your Terms

Later in high school, I was starting at second base for my JV baseball team. My dad and grandfather came to watch. My granddad had played semi-pro ball before becoming a Maryland State Trooper, but dementia was stealing him away, piece by piece. He didn't say much by then, but the light in his eyes was still there.

Late in the game, I blew it. A ground ball was hit to me, and it slipped through my glove, and the other team surged ahead. I stormed into the dugout, slammed my glove down, and felt ready to quit. Then I felt a tap on my shoulder. My grandfather stood behind the fence, frail but steady, and smiled, the same smile I remembered from boyhood.

"Is it over?" he asked.

I looked at him, confused. "No?" I muttered.

"Then grab a bat and end it on your terms." He smiled and winked at me. His words hit like lightning.

Next at-bat, I swung with everything I had and cracked a double. Runners scored; we won the game. I looked back at him and saw a faint nod. That moment stayed with me. My grandfather would pass away a few years later, but his words still echo: when you mess up, it's not the end, it's just a setup for your next swing.

Playing Catch as the Sun Sets

Now I'm a dad. My son, Brooks, named after the great Brooks Robinson[17], is ten. He's never cared much for baseball. Video games and teasing his sister are his world. I'd almost given up hope he'd ever share my love for the game.

Then, on Opening Day this year, the Orioles crushed a big win with six homers. Brooks plopped down beside me, eyes wide, cheering with each blast. After the game, he turned and asked, almost shy: *"Wanna play catch outside?"*

---

[17] Brooks Robinson (1937–2023) was a Hall of Fame third baseman who spent his entire 23-year Major League Baseball career with the Baltimore Orioles. Known as "The Human Vacuum Cleaner" for his defensive brilliance, he won 16 consecutive Gold Glove Awards and helped lead the Orioles to two World Series titles.

My heart nearly exploded. *"Heck yeah!"* I yelled.

Out in the yard, as the sun dropped over the Eastern Shore horizon, we tossed the ball back and forth, his grin growing with each throw. And with every throw, memories rushed back: the sandlot that saved me, the foul ball that taught me about love, my granddad's advice about never giving up.

But this moment was new. Just me and my boy, the ball singing between us. Baseball reminded me that fatherhood isn't forcing your dreams onto your kids, it's sharing moments and letting them build their own. For the first time, I was part of Brooks' baseball story.

In that moment, the weight of the world lifted. Like a quiet escape, the grind of adulthood melted away, and I felt as free as that kid on the sandlot thirty years ago. Maybe that's baseball's final gift, freeing us from the stress of grown-up life, letting us awaken the inner child we thought we'd buried.

I share these stories because every spring, as baseball returns, I'm reminded how much the game means to me, how it shaped me through joy and pain, heartbreak and pride.

And maybe, as you read this, baseball stirs something in you too. Maybe it's playing catch with your dad. Maybe it's the sound of play-by-play on the radio during a long car ride.

Maybe it's a ballpark memory with friends, family, or the one you love. For good or bad, those moments stick. They're threads of nostalgia, joy, ache, hope, reminders of what it means to be alive.

Baseball isn't just a game. It's a heartbeat. A resurrection. A reminder that, yes, hope is a good thing. For me, baseball pulled me out of an abyss, tethered me to something raw and real, and whispered: You're still here. There's still light ahead.

And as spring dawns and baseball blooms again, I hope my son Brooks finds that same light. I hope the game teaches him about friendship, romance, perseverance, and family, just like it did for me.

Because I believe that baseball, this game I love, can save his life like it saved mine. One pitch. One catch. One lesson at a time.

End of Article

PunkRocker HR takeaway from article:

In PunkRocker HR, work should feel kind of like the sandlot, a place where everyone feels like they belong.

Belonging is a powerful thing. When you feel it, it reminds you that you matter, that you have a place in the story. But when it's gone, it can leave a hole that nothing else seems to fill. After rereading that essay, I realized how much I missed that feeling, not just at work, but in life. The sense of being part of something bigger, of knowing my purpose.

Maybe that's what this whole journey was really about. Not just remembering what I'd lost, but finding my way back to it. At a previous organization, when I clashed with a leader that made me feel miserable, I never quite felt that sense of belonging, and that isolation hurt more than I ever admitted at the time. Sitting there that night, reading this article, I thought about my grandfather's words: *"End it on your terms."* For a while, I'd almost let other people's recent actions define the outcome of my leadership story.

But not anymore.

I wanted the next chapter of my HR leadership story to be different. Our teams need us. Our families, our communities, and the people we might lead in the future need us. For me, it was time to stand up, dust myself off, grab my bat, step back up to the plate, and keep swinging, whether I struck out or not. Because that's what leadership, and life, really come down to: choosing to keep playing, even after life throws you a few curveballs.

Call to Action:
What are you doing to make your workplace feel more like a sandlot, a place where everyone belongs and can show up as their authentic self?

Chapter 14: It's a Wonderful Life

After reading that last essay, lying in that field, I felt hope return. I thought about future failures. Yes, I might experience setbacks and misalignments again. Some people might think less of me because of it. But I also sensed there were still successes ahead — the kind that help others despite my mistakes. And that's what I hope you take from my story: regardless of our past, we still have value to offer. We still have a story worth telling.

Nearly two hours had passed as I lay there, letting the words from my articles and essays wash over me. By the end, something had shifted. Like George Bailey in It's a Wonderful Life, running through the streets of Bedford Falls shouting, "I want to live!" I felt an almost absurd urge to shout, "Let's lead with humanity!" I felt a spark of defiance and hope.

In the days that followed, I met with a trusted mentor to talk about my renewed peace and purpose, and the emerging clarity around PunkRocker HR. We discussed learning and growth. He told me, "If you want to give advice to others about how to learn, grow, and lead, remember that it goes both ways. We have to be better at receiving advice and feedback ourselves. Feedback is a gift."

He was right.

And perhaps this was the final piece of the PunkRocker HR picture: PunkRocker HR leaders view feedback, whether giving it or receiving it, as a gift. It's easy to give advice. It takes maturity, self-awareness, and humility to receive it.

Then he asked me, "When was a time in your life when you received feedback and took it personally?"

I paused. After a long silence, one day came back to me — the day of Hurricane Isabel.

Hurricane Isabel

It was September 18, 2003. I was working as a mail carrier in Baltimore. It was already a rainy, windy day, but I hadn't given up on finishing my route. "I'll get it done before the storm really hits," I told myself.

Just as I was about to finish for the day, I stopped at a gas station to fill up my truck. One of my supervisors called, upset about a few misdeliveries on my route. He told me I needed to slow down and remember that accuracy was more important than speed. His tone was condescending, and I could feel myself getting angry.

All I could think was, "Who does this guy think he is? I show up every day on time. I picked up extra routes. I never complain. I make one mistake, and he jumps on me? Here I am out here delivering mail in a hurricane, and he calls not to check on me, but to complain?"

The supervisor had a reputation for being a jerk. Still, I should have seen that the content of his feedback was correct. At that point in my career, I was immature about receiving feedback. Instead of taking it professionally, I took it personally. The call hit me like a freight train. I was angrier than I had ever been. Looking back, I'm embarrassed to admit how silly it was, but I think it was the snowball effect: the stress of working in a storm, the frustration of being called out, and the humbling realization that I wasn't as great as I thought I was.

By the time I reached my last street, the skies had darkened. The wind howled down the narrow blocks, bending tree branches and rattling storm drains. Sheets of rain slapped against me as I pulled the last bag of mail from my truck. Just then, my Postmaster called: "John, we've been ordered to pull all mail carriers off the street. The worst part of the hurricane is about to hit. Get back as soon and as safely as you can."

But I looked down the block at the twelve houses I hadn't delivered yet. The wind had picked up to a roar. Rain stung like needles against my face. I could have left right then. No one would have blamed me.

So, I pushed forward. Step after step, porch after porch, climbing slick stairs, clutching the railing, shoving envelopes through doors as tree limbs cracked above me. I delivered all twelve houses, teeth clenched, heart pounding. By the end, I was drenched, exhausted, and numb.

As I stood by the rear of my mail truck, I heard a faint whimper. Under a fallen branch, a tiny Pomeranian was trembling. I knew him—Howie, from the last house on my route. On normal days, he'd dart out barking and snap at my ankles. But not today. Today, Howie needed me.

I threw my mail satchel into the truck and ran for him. Just as I scooped him up, another massive branch cracked and slammed to the ground behind me, right where I'd been standing seconds before. If I hadn't gone for Howie, that branch would have crushed me. Standing there, soaked to the bone, clutching a shivering little dog who usually hated me, I realized something: Howie didn't just need saving that day. I did.

What I didn't fully understand at the time was this: the supervisor's feedback earlier that day wasn't the enemy. My reaction to it was. Accuracy did matter more than speed. Slowing down would have made me better. But instead of receiving the correction with humility, I let pride take the wheel. The storm outside wasn't the only thing raging. There was one brewing inside me too.

That day taught me something I wouldn't fully appreciate until years later: sometimes the very feedback we resist is the thing meant to steady us.

Connecting the Dots

As I told that story to my mentor, he appreciated my honesty. Then he asked, "Can I give you some feedback now, something that might help you learn from all of this and bring the final pieces of PunkRocker HR together?"

I said yes.

He asked me:

"What could you have done better in your recent role as an HR leader?"

I sat with the question.

Together, we created an After Action Report, also known as an AAR, outlining lessons learned and areas where I could grow. The goal wasn't self-condemnation. It was ownership. That's a practice I recommend to every leader: memorialize setbacks. Own your part. Learn from them.

One piece of feedback he offered was this: my team may have needed an HR leader with stronger relationships with leaders they struggled with. After months of feeling like an outsider with one particular leader, perhaps I gave up too quickly.

Could others have leaned in more as well? Absolutely. But growth requires owning my part.

I could have leaned further into my own principles: grace, curiosity, connection. I could have fought longer for relational bridge-building instead of allowing discouragement to win.

And that was the final lesson.

Feedback is not an attack. It's a gift.

Bringing it Home

Up next are the concluding lessons that emerged from my night in the field and from revisiting the writings that shaped this journey. The final section of this book brings everything full circle by defining PunkRocker HR in full: what it means, how it works, and how we can bring its principles to life in our workplaces and in our leadership.

If you've come this far, perhaps you're willing to come just a little farther and see how this all comes together...

Conclusion: Alien-Humans

Leaving a job where I felt like an outsider and experiencing misalignment where humanity felt turned all the way down, led to the discovery of PunkRocker HR. In this concluding section, I want to wrap things up by answering a few questions you might be asking as we close this story:

1. What is the full definition of PunkRocker HR? What does it look like in action?
2. What if a naysayer doubts whether this concept really makes a "business" impact?
3. Why even bother publishing this book and putting the PunkRocker HR concept out there for criticism?
4. And what happens if we want to live out PunkRocker HR but find ourselves drifting off course, how do we reset to find our way again?

Alien-Human

Earlier in this book, in the chapter titled *Field of Dreams*, I wrote about a scene from the newer *Superman* movie where he admits that his way of seeing and treating others is "the real punk rock." There's another scene later in the movie, near the end (spoiler alert), that has stayed with me even more. Superman is in the final battle with his nemesis, Lex Luthor. As Superman essentially has Lex defeated, Lex lashes out with one last insult:

Lex Luthor: "You piece of **** alien!"

Superman: "That is where you've always been wrong about me, Lex.

…I'm as human as anyone.

…I love, I get scared, I wake up every morning and despite not knowing what to do, I put one foot in front of the other and try to make the best choices I can.

…I screw up all the time. But that's being human. And that's my greatest strength[18]."

That scene moves me every time. It reminds me that as HR professionals and leaders, the corporate world often demands that we be something almost alien—flawless, always strong, always "on." We're expected to straddle the impossible gap: maintaining trust with executives while also being the voice for employees; sitting with people on their worst days even when we're quietly having one ourselves; being seen as failures one day and heroes the next.

In a way, "Alien Human" is the best description I can think of for this role. Superman's words remind me it's okay to screw up. It's okay to not always know what to do. It's okay to admit that we are human. I've lived through that truth: In a former role as an HR leader I did good work, yet still found myself leaving in the end. At times, it felt as if I had to be something close to perfect—almost alien-like, to be accepted by a leader I clashed with. But just like Superman, our humanity isn't our weakness. It's our greatest strength. And that idea sits at the core of PunkRocker HR.

---

[18] Dialogue from Superman (2025), written and directed by James Gunn.

The Definition of PunkRocker HR

To make it simple, I define PunkRocker HR through four core actions — **P.U.N.K.** Each letter captures what it means to turn up the humanity at work and show what this approach *looks like* in action:

P — Protect Humanity: We protect the humanity of the people we lead by fighting for balance, dignity, and respect. Protecting time, peace, and purpose is just as vital as meeting goals. When we get this right, our people don't just leave work finished, they leave with enough peace and purpose to show up as great humans at home too.

U — Unlearn and Understand: We challenge old assumptions and unlearn what no longer serves today's workplace. We stay curious, seek understanding before judgment, and remember that every employee is more than a job title, they're a human with a life beyond the badge. And part of truly understanding people means taking the time to learn how they want to be led, not just how we prefer to lead.

N — Nurture Performance with Purpose: We champion high performance, but never at the expense of a person's well-being. We set clear expectations and hold our teams accountable, but we make sure they have the tools, coaching, and support they need to succeed. We nurture through empathy and purpose, creating an environment where people can grow, contribute, and still have energy left for the people they love at home.

K — Keep It Real: We lead with authenticity, courage, and care. No façades, no corporate masks, just honest connection, even when it's uncomfortable. We keep it real because trust can't grow in the dark.

It's All About Stewardship

Earlier in this book, I shared how I'd explain PunkRocker HR in an elevator pitch. But now that you've read the stories behind it, I can tell you what it truly means. If my college English professor were here, he'd probably say, "Bottom line it—what's the main idea?"

In essence, it comes down to stewardship.

PunkRocker HR is leadership through stewardship of people's humanity at work—so they can go home and be even better humans with their families, their friends, and their communities.

The Thoughtful Pause

There is one simple habit that has helped me become a better steward of the humanity of others — whether I lead them, support them, or simply work beside them. I call it *The Thoughtful Pause.*

Anytime you're about to make a decision, respond to a difficult situation, or say something that could impact someone's dignity, well-being, or livelihood, take a thoughtful pause in the moment. What do I mean by that? Stop for one breath. Take a slow inhale. Then hold for a beat. Then release.

After that pause, walk through the PunkRocker HR checklist at the end of this book to analyze the action you're about to take:

Am I leading with curiosity or with judgment?

Am I showing care or clinging to control?

Some leaders think they have to respond instantly to appear confident and in control. But stewardship isn't about proving how fast or how smart we are. It's about slowing down long enough to honor the humanity in front of us. Taking a thoughtful pause can help you do just that.

The Naysayer in the Room

Of course, any time you talk about leading with stewardship and heart, there will always be skeptics. As I reflect on that scene from *Superman,* I can hear the voice of a leader I once worked with who always said, "If you are making a proposal, you need a naysayer in the room." Someone to poke holes, to force you to sharpen your case. So, let's invite one in here, and I'll name him "Lex."

Lex: PunkRocker HR sounds nice, but where's the proof it actually drives results?

My response: PunkRocker HR is contagious! It works, and not just in data, but in how it spreads.

Are we leading our employees the same way we want them treating our customers? Because here's the truth: when you turn up the volume on humanity in the workplace, that same humanity echoes out to your customers. Employees who feel seen, respected, and cared for don't just perform better, they carry that same care into every customer interaction.

That's the greatest benefit of buying into the PunkRocker HR mission: it's viral in the best way. The empathy, patience, and respect leaders show to their people ripple outward. When employees feel valued, they value others. When they're trusted, they act with trust. When they're treated like humans, they treat customers like humans, too.

Example 1 – Chick-fil-A: Their success isn't just about great food; it's about their *Culture of Care*[19]. From day one, team members are taught to see each guest as a person, not a transaction, to serve with empathy, warmth, and genuine respect. That care starts inside the organization, where employees are supported, mentored, and celebrated. When people feel cared for at work, they naturally care for others. "My pleasure" isn't a script, it's the echo of a culture that values humanity first.

Example 2 – The Ritz-Carlton: Every employee, from housekeeping to management, is trusted with the power to make things right for guests, up to $2,000[20] per incident, no manager approval needed. That level of empowerment reflects deep trust. When employees know they matter, they rise to the moment, creating unforgettable experiences for the people they serve.

So no, PunkRocker HR isn't soft. It's smart. It's strategic empathy in action, leadership that understands the customer experience begins with the employee experience. When we turn up the volume on humanity at work, it doesn't stop at the door. It follows our people home, and it greets every customer who walks through it.

---

[19] Chick-fil-A Culture of Care — Chick-fil-A's Culture of Care emphasizes serving both employees and guests with empathy, dignity, and respect. Source: https://www.chick-fil-a.com/cultureofcare

[20] The Ritz-Carlton $2,000 Rule https://customersthatstick.com/blog/the-ritz-carltons-famous-2000-rule/

Lex: Why should anyone listen to you?

My response: Do we stop listening to any leader who ever experiences a set back? Lou Holtz[21] resigned after one disastrous season coaching the New York Jets in 1976. Most people thought his career was over. But he came back to college football, rebuilt himself, and eventually led Notre Dame to a national championship in 1988. One set back doesn't erase the future, it's about timing, growth, and the right fit.

You're right, I experienced leadership and value misalignment as an HR leader in one previous role. My guess is that some people reading this book has experience that too. I believe that anyone who finds themselves in that situation should remember to embrace the ways you succeeded. When I read the messages from employees and fellow leaders who reached out after I left, thanking me for coaching them, for making the workplace more engaging, for helping them grow. They thanked me for caring about them as human beings, and that told me my impact mattered. Too often, in high-performing cultures, we get so locked in on the fumbles that we forget the touchdowns. But a season isn't defined by one turnover, it's defined by the points you score over time. The truth is, we must hold space for both.

PunkRocker HR isn't about pretending to be perfect. It's about being human enough to admit when you stumble, and then choosing to learn, grow, and keep showing up, with empathy, with courage, and with hope. And that's what I want readers of this book to know: you are

---

[21] Lou Holtz: After resigning from the New York Jets in 1976 following a single disappointing season (3–10 record), he returned to the college game and rebuilt his career. He went on to lead the University of Notre Dame to a national championship in 1988 and became the only coach in NCAA history to guide six different programs to bowl games

more than your setbacks. Your real legacy lies in the human beings who are better for having worked with you, been led by you, or been helped by you. That's where the true success of HR professionals, and leaders, will always live.

That's why I created the PunkRocker HR Checklist at the end of this book—a gut check for all of us. A daily reminder to ask:
- Am I being the calm in the storm or adding to it?
- Am I protecting dignity and balance—or defaulting to policy?

Is the Juice Worth the Squeeze?

As I wrote the closing to this book, I went back to the field where I discovered PunkRocker HR a few months ago. This time, though, I returned with my children, Brooks and Zoey. The field sits next to a playground, separated by a long fence. It was sunset, late in September. I sat in the field watching them play, laptop in my lap, trying to figure out how to end this book. And the thought hit me: Should I even publish this? Who would care if I did?

Recently, a coworker I coached decades ago at the post office, who has since been promoted to a leadership role there, posted on Facebook celebrating a significant career milestone. I commented to congratulate her. She messaged me back and said:

> "Thanks so much for your coaching all those years ago. I probably wouldn't be where I'm at if it wasn't for you. I still hear your voice in those tough moments, reminding me to consider 'Is the juice worth the squeeze?'"

When I think about this phrase I've used so often, I'm reminded of an event that took place just a few months before I left my role as HR leader at this previous organization. I was sitting on a Q&A panel with three other leaders, answering questions from a room full of emerging leaders in a program I was facilitating. One asked me a question I completely forgot about when I was in my "Pit" after resigning from my job:

> Emerging Leader: "How do you hold true to your personal values as a leader when you have to make a tough decision required by your job that may cause you to choose between your personal values and your job?"

I paused and answered like this:

> "It's all about priorities and hierarchies in life. At the top of my priorities is my relationship with God and my faith. Second is my relationship with my wife and children. Third is my role as a leader here at this organization. When I have to make a tough decision, I consider how that decision could impact those relationships. I have to leave my job at the end of the day with enough peace to give my all to the relationships higher up that list. That often helps guide me in that decision."

The emerging leader pressed further: "So what if your decision might go against what your boss wants? It looks like that might be at the bottom of that hierarchy. What do you do?

I replied: "We all value the important work we do here. Our work does matter, it's how we provide for our families. That said, the hard truth is this: we are all replaceable at work. I know that stings to say, but it's true. However, we are not replaceable at home with our families. That's why the hierarchy is important. When you have to make a decision in that situation, you consider the hierarchy in your life, and you've got to ask yourself this: is the juice worth the squeeze?"

So here I sit, asking the same question. *Is the juice worth the squeeze* to publish this book? Maybe someone out there, burned out, defeated, or standing in their own field, is waiting for a reason to keep going. If this book helps even one person, then yes, the juice is worth the squeeze.

As I looked up from the laptop, my kids were looking at me.

"What are you doing, nerd?" my daughter yelled. "Put down the laptop and come play with us!"

And that's when it hit me. I don't know what the future holds. But I've learned more from failure than from any success. I'm still here. I choose to show up, for my kids, my family, and the people I lead. Because it's worth it. The juice is worth the squeeze.

Perspective and Forgiveness

Hopefully, you're ready to join me on the PunkRocker HR journey. It won't always be easy, some days it will feel messy, and it's natural to drift off course from time to time. The real question is, when that happens, how do we reset the PunkRocker HR "GPS" and find our way back on track?

As you've read through this book and the many stories, I'm sure you've identified some potential "villains" along the way, both past and present. When I was talking with a mentor about this, he told me something I'll never forget:

> "I don't care how good a person you think you are; we all play the villain in someone's story."

Ouch. But he's right. I'd like to think if you surveyed 100 people, 9 out of 10 would say I've been a good person, maybe even a coach or mentor to them at some point. But I'm also sure, even with the best of intentions, there are a few who would say I fell short, and maybe even see me as a villain in their story. That stings, but it's an important perspective. None of us are as perfect as we might think we are, and that truth sits right at the core of our humanity.

I also think about those who may have played the villain in my stories. If you surveyed 100 people about them, chances are 9 out of 10 would say those individuals are not villains at all, but rather great mentors or even heroes in their lives. Again, it's perspective.

That's why this final lesson matters so much. I've chosen to forgive those who, whether intentionally or not, played the role of villain in my story. Truly forgive them and release them from my heart. That includes the leader from Chapter 1 that I clashed with. I forgive them fully and pray that God blesses them, and that one day, they feel inspired to turn the volume back up on humanity for the people they lead. Because for better or worse, they're human too, just like me, doing their best to navigate this complicated journey of life.

Forgiveness, when combined with our humanity, is both heroic and deeply human. And I hope that anyone I've ever hurt—or anyone for whom I've played the villain—can forgive me, too.

I'm reminded of another great quote from Ted Lasso:

> "I hope that either all of us or none of us are judged by the actions of our weakest moments, but rather the strength we show when and if we're ever given a second chance."

When I think of our PunkRocker HR GPS system in our lives, sometimes it glitches, we lose our way, and we need to hit "reboot." Forgiveness is how we reboot that GPS. Forgiveness forces us to humble ourselves in a deeply human way, and it's not always easy. But it's worth it. And once the GPS comes back online, we're faced with the question: where to next? That's where hope steps in. Hope helps us set the new destination.

Hold on to Hope

When I think about living out PunkRocker HR as leaders at work or at home, it's important to remember that hope is at the center of this approach. Hope allows us to see the humanity in others and approach our work and life with empathy, compassion, and a fight for balance, for the people we work with and the people we live with. But it can be easy to lose hope at times, especially in the traditional corporate world, when our approach is rejected or dismissed.

As I consider this concept of hope, I reflect for a moment. I see my kids motioning for me to come play, I set aside my laptop and join them as the sun sets in the background, their laughter and jokes making me feel alive again.

I push my daughter on the swing...

My son shoots down the slide, laughing like the world is brand new…

We sit on a park bench together, scrolling through Instagram reels, cracking up as the sky fades to orange.

And in that small, ordinary moment, I realize how far I've come. I'm standing on the same field where, just months earlier, I questioned my purpose and wondered if my best days as a leader were already behind me. But after looking back on my life through those old essays, writing this book, and now sitting here surrounded by their joy, I felt hope return in full. I made it. Like leaders before us who have experienced misalignment and setbacks, our stories still have chapters to be written.

That's when it hit me: whether you work in HR or not, whether you carry a formal title or not, hope is what inspires people to turn up the volume on humanity — at work, at home, and in our communities.

And when I think back to the story I shared in Chapter One, and what happened to me at a previous organization, I finally understand why I needed to tell it. I used to wish it had never happened. But now? I'm thankful for it. Here's why:

Perhaps the most human thing we can do is take the very thing that almost broke us, the thing that could have left us in the dark and turn it into something…beautiful…something that gives hope to others.

As I close this book, I want to leave you with a call to action that has carried me through. A reminder that the work we do matters, that the people we lead are worth fighting for, and that our presence, both at work and at home, can be a beacon of light[22]:

"It's easy to feel hopeful on a beautiful day like today...

but there will be dark days ahead of us to...

there will be days when you feel all alone...

and that's when hope is needed most...

no matter how buried it gets or how lost you feel...

you must promise me that you will hold on to hope, keep it alive...

we have to be greater than what we suffer...

*my wish for you, is to become **hope,** people need that...*

and even when we fail...what better way is there to live?"

---

[22] Gwen Stacy, The Amazing Spider-Man 2 (Sony Pictures, 2014)

PunkRocker HR Checklist

Use this anytime you're facing a big decision, tough situation, or critical task.

Slogan	Reflective Question
In PunkRocker HR, we don't just process hires and exits by the book, we do it by the heart.	Is the decision you're considering being made with heart, or just by the book?
In PunkRocker HR, we are the calm in the storm.	In the task you're tackling, are you adding to the storm, or choosing to be the calm others can hold onto?
In PunkRocker HR, we don't measure leadership by control, we measure it by care.	Is the decision you're making about clinging to control, or showing care that people will remember long after policies fade?
In PunkRocker HR, we look for the silver linings.	As you approach this challenge, are you pausing long enough to notice the silver linings that could give you and others the strength to keep going?
Hope is human. In PunkRocker HR, we fight to keep it alive.	In the task you're facing, are you keeping your distance with sympathy or standing with people in empathy and hope?
In PunkRocker HR, we don't just say thanks, we show authentic appreciation.	Does the decision you're considering include space to show authentic appreciation not just for what someone does, but for who they are?
In PunkRocker HR, we honor time as the greatest gift, especially the time employees spend with their families.	Will the decision or task you're tackling show employees you value their time or just the time they give to work?
In PunkRocker HR, we know that true strength comes from vulnerability.	In this moment, are you willing to let your humanity show — or are you hiding behind perfection?
In PunkRocker HR, we choose curiosity over judgment, every time.	In your decision, are you leaning into curiosity or being judgmental and sticking with the status quo?
In PunkRocker HR, the real measure of success is employees going home with peace and purpose.	Will the task or decision you're facing help people go home with peace and purpose or leave them drained and empty?
In PunkRocker HR, bridging the gap means putting ourselves in the other person's shoes — every time, even when it hurts.	In this decision, are you truly stepping into a coworker's shoes — not just to understand their role, but to understand what they value and how they want to be led?
In PunkRocker HR, we don't allow ourselves to be the victim, we seize the opportunity to be heroes for others.	In the setback or challenge you're facing, are you seeing yourself as the victim or using it as an opportunity to help others climb out of their Pit?

Photo Gallery:

John as Doc Brown from Chapter 1: "Field of Dreams"

John in his Mail Carrier uniform from Chapter 2: "Hey, Mr. Postman."

Brooks from Chapter 8: "The Grinch."

Brooks and the Honorary
Contract from Chapter 5:
"The Silver Lining."

John and Zoey from Chapter 6:
"Hope is a Good Thing."

John and Sharon
from Chapter 6,
"Hope is a Good
Thing."

The "I'm kind of a big deal" sign form Chapter 7: "Authentic Appreciation."

John and his dad from Chapter 13: "Sandlot Salvation."

John in his Howard High baseball uniform from Chapter 10: "Lessons in Leadership and Vulnerability."

Epilogue (Post-Credit Scene)

If superhero movies have taught us anything, it's that the story isn't really over when the credits roll. There's always a post-credits scene. Think of this chapter as just that. You've heard my story, the climb out of the pit, the lessons learned, the call to lead with hope and humanity. But there's one more bonus scene worth watching, one that looks ahead to the generation that will one day inherit our workplaces: Generation Alpha.

Workforce of the Future
Driving home from work not long ago, I decided to check in on my 14-year-old daughter, Zoey. I gave her a call. Instead of picking up, she sent me straight to voicemail and shot back a text: "What?"

At first, the millennial dad in me felt a mix of irritation and jealousy. Back in the early '90s, we didn't have cell phones, we had one clunky rotary phone on the kitchen wall, and if you missed a call, you missed it. But once I got past the sting of her "what?" reply, I realized this wasn't meant to be disrespectful (it did still sting). It was a glimpse into her generation's world. Gen Alpha prefers quick texts over long phone calls, even with Dad.

That tiny moment reminded me of something important: if I want to reach this generation, I have to adjust how I connect. And if we, as leaders, want to prepare for them in the workplace, we have to do the same.

Defining Gen Alpha

My journey with Gen Alpha began in July 2011 when Zoey was born. A few years later, my son Brooks joined the ranks in 2014. They're among the earliest Alphas, kids born between 2011 and 2025. They've grown up in the shadow of the COVID-19 pandemic and in a world where iPads, TikTok, and AI aren't innovations, they're the air they breathe.

One moment, I catch them choreographing a TikTok dance. The next, they're cracking each other up with the card game "Kids Against Maturity." Brooks even runs his own YouTube channel, reminding family members to "like and subscribe." These quirks aren't just kid stuff; they're shaping the values and habits of a generation that will soon walk through our office doors. What follows isn't an exhaustive list, but a reflection of my own experiences and research into Gen Alpha. These are a few things worth keeping in mind as they grow up, step into the workforce, and begin defining who they are for themselves.

What Strengths Gen Alpha Might Bring
Gen Alpha won't just use technology, they'll shape it. Tech fluency and innovation will come naturally to them. They're wildly creative too, already editing videos, curating online communities, and finding imaginative ways to solve problems.

Attending elementary school during COVID forced them to adapt early. They learned how to pivot fast, and that adaptability will stick with them. They'll expect employers to care about these things. And perhaps most striking, they're comfortable with their voice. Social platforms have already given them a microphone, and they'll expect to be heard at work.

Potential Weaknesses (and Opportunities for Leaders)
Of course, every strength comes with its flip side. Some Alphas might struggle with short attention spans after a childhood of constant stimulation. Others might lean so heavily on technology that face-to-face conversations feel foreign. They're used to instant gratification, everything at the touch of a button. Patience and persistence will need to be taught and modeled. With so much information at their fingertips, they'll also need guidance in finding meaning, not just content. Leaders will need to normalize conversations about mental health and create safety nets for resilience.

Preferences for Skilled Trades and Gig Work
Another shift we'll see is in career choices. With college debt on the rise and AI threatening many white-collar jobs, Gen Alpha may look toward skilled trades (after decades of Gen X and Millennials being told a college education is the only way). Apprenticeships and vocational training could feel more practical than four years of debt. Trades that rely on creativity, craftsmanship, and problem-solving will still matter in an automated world.

And don't expect them to stick to the traditional nine-to-five path. Many will dive headfirst into the gig economy, rideshare in the morning, freelance design in the afternoon, and YouTube creation at night. For traditional employers, this will be a challenge. For leaders willing to embrace flexibility, it's an opportunity.

What Leaders Can Do Now

So how do we prepare? It's not about flashy programs. It's about leaning into the same human traits that pulled me out of my own pit: empathy, balance, voice, and humanity. We need to consider employee benefits that reflect these values.

Lead with empathy by caring about more than output. Protect balance by modeling healthy boundaries and refusing to run people dry. Amplify voices by creating space for contributions, not just compliance. Champion mental health by making it safe to say, "I'm not okay." And above all, model humanity, not perfection. Gen Alpha doesn't want flawless superheroes. They want real leaders who stumble, learn, and keep showing up.

Like Superman embracing his human side, we must lead Gen Alpha with heart, not systems. The PunkRocker HR Checklist of empathy, balance and voice, prepares us for Gen Alpha's arrival. Are you ready for the next scene?

Author's Note

If you've made it this far, thank you. Thank you for walking through my stories, for sitting with the hard moments, and for sharing in the hope that carried me out of the pit. Writing this book was never about being perfect or polished, it was about being real, being human, and putting something into the world that might help someone else.

If even one story here gave you strength or reminded you that you're not alone in this work or in life, then it was worth writing.

So, here's my ask: take what you've read, wrestle with it, make it your own, and pass it forward. The world doesn't need more perfect leaders. It needs more human ones. Leaders who are willing to show up, scars and all, and still choose empathy, courage, and hope.

That's the heartbeat of PunkRocker HR. And my hope is that you'll keep turning up the volume on humanity and hope, at work, at home, and everywhere in between.

—John